The Abduction of
of
Richard Neal

A Story seldom told

Anthony Morris

∞ INFINITY
PUBLISHING

ISBN 978-1-4958-0958-3

Published December 2015

INFINITY PUBLISHING
1094 New DeHaven Street, Suite 100
West Conshohocken, PA 19428-2713
Toll-free (877) BUY BOOK
Local Phone (610) 941-9999
Fax (610) 941-9959
Info@buybooksontheweb.com
www.buybooksontheweb.com

The nucleus of this historic narrative is
drawn from the archival files of my family,
passed to me and my siblings in old
black tin document boxes, albums, musty
wooden crates and cardboard cartons.

In compiling such a document as this, dealing
so largely with facts and dates, perfect accuracy
is difficult to achieve, due to different points
of view, etc. although great pains have been
taken to make it as correct as possible.

*Text in italics indicates direct
transcription of original documents.*

Caspar Morris, M.D.
1882
AGE 79

PREFACE

Since I was a young boy, I have long been fascinated by the story of a black slave who had been owned by James Cheston, the father of my great great grandmother Anne (Cheston) Morris. This slave was freed by Anne and her husband, Dr. Caspar Morris, in 1844, almost twenty years before the American Civil War.

As I move into what I consider to be the latter years of my life, I feel compelled to finish what my grandfather started to do over 100 years ago. That is, to bring together and put down on paper all the different pieces of this story. It is the story of a freed black man's struggles to keep his family together.

My greatest fear is that, when I am gone, those that follow will not realize the depth and importance of this story. I fear that they will only see musty meaningless old papers, and that these records could too easily be lost forever.

TABLE OF CONTENTS

CAST OF PEOPLE IN THIS NARATIVE
in order of appearance

<u>Richard Neal</u> (Neale?) "Dicky" - former slave of James Cheston family of Ivy Neck, West River, Ann Arundel County, MD., freed Nov.10, 1844 at age 33 ±.

<u>Matilda Neal</u> - wife of Richard Neal - slave of Capt. Mayo.

<u>Their six children</u>: - William - age 15, Rachael - age 14, plus Mary, Emeline, James, and Catherine (ages unknown).

<u>Commodore Isaac Mayo</u> - captain, U.S. Navy - former owner of Matilda Neal and her children. Commander of the USS Constitution, flag ship of the African Squadron.

<u>James Cheston family</u> - former owners of Richard Neal and John Davis plus 75 other slaves.

<u>Ann (Cheston) Morris</u> - daughter of James Cheston Jr., wife of Dr. Casper Morris.

Dr. Casper Morris - husband of Ann Cheston Morris.

Townsend Sharpless - employer of Richard Neal in Philadelphia.

Mr. Slaughter - slave dealer to whom Commodore Mayo sold Matilda and her children in Baltimore.

Mr. Gordon - a slave trader from Tennessee who buys Matilda and her children in Baltimore.

Mr. Francis King - a leading Baltimore Quaker who acted as an agent for Dr. Morris in purchasing Richard Neal's family's freedom.

Mr. Bollion - a slave trader at Richmond, VA, who purchases the rest of the children.

William Hunter - a slave of Commodore Mayo who swore out an affidavit against Richard Neal.

Enoch Louis Lowe - governor of Maryland who issued request for arrest and extradition of Richard Neal, to the governor of PA.

William Bigler - governor of PA who issued warrant for the arrest of Richard Neal.

John Lamb - of Annapolis, agent from Maryland for Commodore Mayo.

Charles Tapper and officer Briest - arresting officers from the Philadelphia Marshall's police.

Billy Green - one of the police officers in the coach from Philadelphia to Chester.

Isaiah Mirkle - Chester police officer assisted the party from the Goff Hotel to the Chester railroad station.

John Davis - former slave of the Cheston family, related to Richard Neal.

Y.S. Walters - abolition proprietor of the "Delaware County Republican", attested to the legitimacy of Gov. Bigler's requisition.

Thomas Garrett - from Wilmington, DE, on train car platform at Chester, he was credited with assisting over 2500 fugitives to flee slavery.

William B. Reed - district attorney at Philadelphia.

Campbell - attorney general.

Chief Justice Jeremiah S. Black, and Judges Ellis Lewis, Walter H. Lowrie and George W. Woodward - Supreme Court Judges at Philadelphia.

Charles Gilpin - mayor of Philadelphia.

William L. Hirst - lawyer for Commodore Mayo.

Peter McCall - lawyer, former mayor of Philadelphia, mildly pro-slavery, consultant to Dr. Morris.

Francis R. Wharton - (later Rev. Wharton), lawyer, also mildly pro-slavery.

James Covert & John Montgomery - Philadelphia officers of the City Police at Chester.

Phineas Pemberton Morris - cousin of Dr. Caspar Morris, lawyer at Philadelphia.

Galloway Cheston Morris - son of Dr. Casper & Ann Cheston Morris (my great grandfather).

LOCATIONS

"GRESHAM" at Mayo Neck, Edgewater, Anne Arundel County, MD. - home and plantation of Commodore Isaac Mayo.

"BLANDAIR" at Elkridge, Howard County, MD. - another of Mayo's plantations near Baltimore.

"IVY NECK" at West River, Anne Arundel County, MD - one of the Cheston family plantations, built by James Cheston in 1785, with an addition in 1858 by Dr. Casper and Ann (Cheston) Morris.

Chapter 1

RICHARD NEAL - THE SLAVE

In 1641, Massachusetts became the first colony in America to legalize slavery, Maryland became the third colony in 1663. By the 1700s, slavery in early genteel Maryland had become greatly different from that of the harsher deep south.

Slavery in the 1700 & 1800s was a normal part of the economy, both in the Northern and the Southern States. It was more so in the South due to the agricultural nature of its economy and the larger landholdings per capita.

Some of the first slaves in America were not Africans but white European convicts, or indentured persons, people who bound themselves to periods of servitude in exchange for room, board, and payment of their passage to this country and, in many cases, never were able to work their way out of debt, so they remained in bondage all their life.

In Maryland, the plantations were generally smaller in size and more commonly called "farms". They were their own little self-sustaining communities. Many owners' families worked side- by-side in the fields with a small work force of slaves. Their product was mainly grain and tobacco, but not cotton.

As these farms grew, the demand for cheap unskilled labor grew rapidly. Landowners quickly turned to the African slave market for manpower.

There was a great discrepancy in the treatment of ones slaves between the middle Atlantic states of Delaware, Maryland and Virginia, and those of the states deeper south. Life expectance of a slave in the fields of the deep South could easily be as little as three years, so the threat of being sent deeper south always hung over the heads of the slaves of the middle Atlantic states. The demand for unskilled labor was much greater prior to Eli Whitney and the Industrial Revolution. Between 1800 and the Civil War great social, moral and economic changes took place, both in the United States and in Europe.

Prior to the American Revolution, there where almost 1,500 slaves in the Quaker city of Philadelphia. By 1790, that number had dropped to less than 300, due mainly to the number of slaves who went over to the British on the promise of freedom. By 1820, there were only seven slaves left in the city and, as much as 10% of the city's total population, were free African/Americans.

In 1829 Caspar Morris, my great great grandfather, a prominent young Philadelphia physician, married Anne Cheston, daughter of a well to do

Baltimore milling merchant, and thus begins my association with RICHARD NEAL (sometimes spelled Neale) - a former slave of Anne's father, James Cheston Jr.

Very little has come to light of Richard Neal's early life as a slave. We do know he was born at "Ivy Neck", a small plantation owned by the Cheston family. It is located on a point of land between the Rhode and the West Rivers which empty into the Chesapeake Bay below Annapolis, near the little town of Galesville, Maryland.

Ivy Neck - West River, MD. - 1850's [4]

No picture of Richard Neal has ever been found.

What we do know is that Richard Neal was born around 1810, and his mother was one of the confidential slaves on the Cheston property. His father was a confidential slave of the Honorable Virgil Maxey.

But what was his mother's name? Was she purchased by the Chestons, or was she inherited by Ann Galloway Cheston? Was she brought to "Ivy Neck" from nearby "Tulip Hill" when Ann and her husband James Cheston built "Ivy Neck"? What was Richard Neal's father's name?

There were a total of seventy seven slaves on the property by 1843. Richard was around 33 years old at this time. Some of the slaves had last names, others did not. Only four of the female slaves were of age to be Richard's mother. None of these four women were given last names. So which one was his mother?

The earliest recollections of Richard Neal that I have found are those of my great grandfather, Galloway Cheston Morris [2]. He recalls in his memoirs, tagging along behind Richard Neal as he went about his chores as a slave on one of the family farms in the early1840's. It was a 690 acre farm, "Ivy Neck", at West River, MD. He remembers "Dicky" carrying him about on his shoulders, and how he taught him to fish, skip stones, etc.

Chapter 2

CHESTON / MORRIS FAMILY - OWNERS

D r. Caspar Morris (1805-1884)[3], was the son of Israel W. and Mary (Hollingsworth) Morris, both of old Philadelphia Quaker families who arrived in Philadelphia in 1682 from London, England.

When Caspar Morris was a young boy, he showed early tastes and proclivities toward medicine. He entered medical school at the University of Pennsylvania in 1819. Upon graduating in 1826, he sailed as a ship's surgeon and supercargo (owners representative onboard) on the ship "Pacific" to India in May 1827. During the long hours at sea, he busied him self in serious studies of Greek and Roman history and mythology. At the same time, his spiritual nature was deeply awakened. He returned to Philadelphia in June of 1828. He deeply and widely immersed his life in medical institutions throughout the city, as well as a large private practice, much of it serving the poor. Dr. Morris contributed largely to general and medical literature, publishing many books, both medical and general in nature. His professional and religious life were blended into a rare harmony.

Although Caspar Morris was born in an old Quaker family, his adult life turned to the Episcopal faith. He was prominent in most of the philanthropic institutions of the time in Philadelphia, and was very much responsible for the establishment of the Episcopal Hospital of Philadelphia, as well as the Church of the Epiphany at the corner of Chestnut and 15th Street, and the Pennsylvania Institute for the Blind.

Anne (Cheston)Morris [1b]   Dr. Caspar Morris [3]

Caspar Morris and Anne Cheston (1810-1880) were married in Baltimore in November 1829. They had 4 children who would live to maturity; Dr. James Cheston Morris (1831-1923), Israel Wistar Morris (1833-1909), Mary Hollingsworth Morris (1835-1919), and Galloway Cheston Morris (1837-1909).

Children - Galloway C., Mary H., I.
Wistar & J. Cheston Morris[1b]

1850's Morris residence - 1428
Chestnut Street, Philadelphia, PA[5]

Anne Cheston was born in Anne Arundel County, Maryland, and was the fourth of eleven children born to James Cheston Jr. (1779-1843) and Mary Ann Hollingsworth (1784-1835). Her father was a prominent merchant of Baltimore, largely engaged in the milling business, the shipment of flour to South America, and importation of coffee in return. He also owned several farms in the West River district of Maryland.

James Cheston, Jr. [1b]

Anne's great grandfather, Dr. Daniel Cheston (1712-1758) of Bristol, England, had arrived in America around 1720 and settled in Kent County, MD. He married the widow, Francina Augustina

Frisby Stevenson (1719-1766), in 1742. They had three children: James Cheston (1747-1798), Francina Augustina Cheston (1750-1825), and Daniel Cheston II (1754-??).

James Cheston married Anne Galloway (1755-1837), daughter of Samuel Galloway of "Tulip Hill", West River, MD, in 1775. James and Anne (Galloway) Cheston with their three children; Daniel Cheston (1776-1811), Francina Augustina Cheston (1777-1857), and James Cheston Jr. (1779-1843), lived with her parents at Tulip Hill for twelve years. They then built and moved to "Ivy Neck" after Anne's father Samuel Galloway, died.

"Tulip Hill" - Galloway residence
- West River, MD [1b]

"Ivy Neck" - Cheston residence -
front view -West River, MD [1b]

"Ivy Neck" - river side

CHAPTER 3

MAYO/BLAND FAMILY[6] [7]

M atilda was a slave at "Gresham" house on the neighboring plantation, "Mayo's Neck", owned by Isaac and Sara (Bland) Mayo.

"Gresham" - Mayo residence
at Mayo's Neck, MD [1a]

"Gresham", a large two and a half story frame dwelling was built around 1686 on land on the South River owned by Captain Edward Selby. It was purchased by Joseph Mayo in 1705. Joseph's son, Isaac Mayo, inherited the 240 acre "Mayo's Neck" plantation between the South and the Rohde rivers, and it next passed on to his son, Isaac Mayo Jr.

Commodore Isaac Mayo Jr. [9]
Painting attributed to Benjamin West

Isaac Mayo Jr. (1794?-1861) was born in Anne Arundel County, MD. Other sources show 1791 as Isaac's birth date. His father had been a Revolutionary War soldier, as were his six uncles. By 1860, then Commodore Mayo had increased his plantation holdings to 1400 acres. The "Gresham" house was restored in 1984 and now is a national landmark.

Isaac Mayo Jr. received an appointment as a midshipman in 1809. As a young naval prodigy, by the age of 18 he was awarded the Congressional Medal of Honor. He would fight valiantly in three wars: the War of 1812 where he was awarded the Medal of Valor by congress; the Seminole War

1835-1842; the Mexican War; and at Vera Cruz, as well as numerous other prominent military engagements. He was wounded twice.

In 1845, he was a prime mover in the establishment of the U.S. Naval Academy at Annapolis. He was a very prominent and well respected officer, a hero of the United States Navy. An obelisk in his honor stands in the cemetery at the Naval Academy.

On December 9, 1852, by now Commodore Mayo, a slave holder himself, he would take command of the African Squadron.

The duties of the African Squadron were the suppression of the African slave trade, tracking down slave ships off the coast of Africa. His flag ship was the 44-gun, three-mast frigate USS Constitution - "Old Ironsides". The USS Constitution had a crew of 450, some were Negroes. At that time, black seamen were known as "Black Jacks".

U.S.S. Constitution [10]

On April 17, 1855, Isaac Mayo is relieved of command of the African Squadron when the U.S.S. Constitution was decommissioned, and after a three months leave, he returned to the naval academy.

The U.S.S. Constitution was refurbished and re-commissioned. She is now the world's oldest commissioned warship still afloat today.

In 1833, Isaac Mayo Jr. married Sarah Battaile Fitzhugh Bland (1808-1885), daughter of Theodoric and Sarah (Glen) Bland, owners of "Blandair" plantation at Elkridge, MD. Her father was a federal judge and Chancellor of Maryland. Mrs. Mayo inherited "Blandair" in 1846. Isaac and Sarah had one child, Sarah Battaile Mayo. Young Sarah Mayo was given "Blandair" plantation as a wedding present upon her marriage to Thomas Henry Gaither in1857. Ten years later, it was sold.

The little town of Mayo, originally known as "Scrabbletown", below Annapolis, was renamed in honor of Commander Mayo.

The slave girl, Matilda, at the neighboring "Mayo's Neck" plantation, had been purchased by Sarah (Glen) Bland from a James Smith, and was sent to live with Mrs. Bland's daughter, Sarah, and son-in-law Captain Isaac Mayo Jr., at their plantation home, "Gresham".

There was a very distinct hierarchy between the slaves of the field and those with trades such as carpenters, blacksmiths, watermen and house servants. Matilda was evidently considered of a higher grade as she was one of the house girls.

Some time around 1829, Richard Neal, from the "Ivy Neck" family of slaves, began courting and married the slave girl, Matilda, of the "Mayo's Neck" plantation.

In Matilda Neal's affidavit taken on Feb. 5th, 1853, [1c] she states:

> "...... *After I was married I lodged with my children in my own quarters. My husband supplied us with flour, tea, coffee, and sugar, in the fall laid up meat of his own raising. One pound of sugar was allowed a week for my family from my master, and I used to get the spent Tea Leaves from the Great House every other night. The servants were allowed the Coffee grounds; but I never asked for them. My Master generally treated me very well. When my Mistress was raised she ordered me whipped, but generally speaking she was kind to me. The overseer did the whipping with the cow-skin; generally 25 lashes. The marks sometimes remained for weeks; sometimes brought blood. Capt Mayo sold two of the servants that came by his wife a few weeks before I ran away; they were a mother and daughter. The mother (daughter) sold from the upper place on Elk Ridge; the mother from the lower one, at West River. The daughter was threatened to be whipped, and hid herself in the*

house. I was there at the time. I understood that the same happened with the mother at the lower place but she did not go off the farm. I understood they were sold for running out of the way of being whipped. I was often threatened with being sold, when my mistress was in a passion. I often told my husband I would have to leave, that I was badly treated and could not stand it and had not been used to it. He would tell me I had better knock along and try to make out. He advised me to be humble. That if I was to run I would be overtaken and sold where I would never see him nor the children again. He always gave me good advise and try to make out the best way I could. I always told him I would go and was bound to go, as I would rather be sold than stay, for of latter years they had got so hard I could not live with them. He scolded me for saying so often and over, and said if I did so he would be blamed for it. ....".

There is no doubt that Captain Mayo was a Naval hero, but his actions against Richard Neal and his family will show a totally different character.

Chapter 4

Neal - A Free Blackman

J ames Cheston Jr. was a staunch Quaker, from a long line of Quakers. Even so, his family had been slave holders for generations before him. Many Quakers, both sides of the Mason - Dixon Line were slave holders. James Cheston Jr., at the time of his death, May 31st, 1843, of a sudden attack of Apoplexy, owned 77 slaves.

In many cases, trusted slaves developed close relationships with their masters and mistresses. This appears to be the case with those of the Cheston family.

For many years, James Cheston Jr. had wished to free all his slaves but feared that they would not be able to survive on their own, because they depended on their masters all their lives. He had freed some of his slaves, those he felt would be capable of self support.

On his death bed in May of 1843, he dictated to his son-in-law, Dr. Caspar Morris, a will leaving all of the slaves to his son, Galloway Cheston, in order that Galloway might carry out his intention of setting all his slaves free. Since this will was nuncupative, (declared orally, as opposed to written) and only witnessed by a family member, it was set aside by the courts. The estate was to be divided, shared and shared alike, between the heirs of James Cheston, Jr.

Slaves were considered property. They could be rented out or mortgaged to raise money. In order to settle the estate, an appraisal of all the slaves had to be made, including those that he had previously, unofficially freed.

Distribution of the Slaves of the Estate of James Cheston

We the subscribers have reappraised the Servants of the late James Cheston, deceased, 77 in number and amounting to $14,623.00. We have also distributed them in 6 lots, awarding one Lot to each of the persons entitled there to:

Lot No. 1. to Jas. Cheston:

Ben	Aged	70	$ 1
Seymour	"	56	50
Ben	"	48	300
Edwd. Neale	"	22	300
Geo. Hobbs	"	24	400
Jno. Wilson	"	20	400
Jas. Smith	"	9	200
Bet	"	50	50
Kitty Neale	"	23	300
Charolotte	"	15	300
Sally Smith	"	3	50
Sophy Carroll	"	8	100
			$ 2451

Lot No. 2. to Galloway Cheston:

Harry	Aged	70	$ 1
Isaac	"	54	20
Anthony	"	40	300
Chas. Bins *	"	24	250
Sam Matthews	"	20	400
Henry Wilson	"	18	400
Wm. Neale	"	2	100
Maria	"	52	50
Prissy	"	44	1
Beckey	"	22	300
Mary Hobbs	"	17	300
Sam Talbot	"	12	100
Rachal Carroll	"	8	100
Moses *	"	47	100
			$ 2422

Lot No. 3. to Samuel Cheston

		Aged	$	
Mat		68	$	1
Peter *	"	49		100
Casam *	"	45		300
Toby Bins *	"	23		400
Thos. Matthews	"	18		400
Jerry	"	15		400
Wm. Bins	"	3		100
Nellie Hobbs	"	50		50
Jane	"	33		100
Rachal Hobbs	"	23		150
Susan	"	16		300
Sophy Davis	"	5		75
Ellen Hobbs	"	3		50
John H. Smith	"	18 mos		50
				$ 2426

Lot No. 4 to Ann Morris

		Aged	$	
George *		64	$	1
William *	"	40		300
Richard Neale *	"	33		400
John Davis	"	24		400
Long Ned	"	32		100
Little Sam	"	10		200
Wm. Neale of Kitty	"	2		100
Daniel Davis	"	28		400
Jenny Smith *	"	40		1
Julia	"	20		300
Fanny	"	16		150
Ellen Wilson	"	9		100
				$ 2452

Lot No. 5 to E. H. Cheston

		Aged	$	
Phil		60	$	20
Jas Bryan	"	50		250
Dan. Neale	"	30		400
Ewd. Carter *	"	22		400
Henry Davis	"	14		350
Chloe Neale	"	18 mos		20
Priss	"	78		1
Nelly	"	22		300
Louisa	"	25		300
Maria Smith	"	11		150
Jane Davis	"	3		50
James Hobbs	"	9		200
				$ 2446

Lot No. 6 to Daniel Murray

		Aged	$	
London		58	$	50
Sam Bryan	"	38		250
Thos. Neal *	"	26		400
Charles	"	16		400
Wm. Hobbs	"	12		300
Richard Carter	"	8		200
Richard Talbot	"	6 mos		25
Rachal	"	60		1
Mary Jane	"	20		300
Eliza	"	17		300
Sophy Smith	"	7		100
Sophy Talbot	"	3		50
Phillia	"	49		50
				$ 2426

	Contains		Servants,	amount	$	
Lot No. 1		12	"	"	$	2451
Lot No. 2	"	14	"	"		2422
Lot No. 3	"	14	"	"		2426
Lot No. 4	"	12	"	"		2452
Lot No. 5	"	12	"	"		2446
Lot No. 6	"	13	"	"		2426
					$	14,623

$ 2437.25 would be the exact portion of each party.

(signed)   J. Thomas.
Alfred Sellman.

Note. (*) denotes those manumitted early.

All were manumitted before the Civil War.

This list [1a] gives the name, age, and appraised value of each individual slave. It also shows the equal division of the slaves, by value, between each of the five living Cheston children plus his grandson, Daniel Murray, son of Dr. James H. Murray and Mary Hollingsworth (Morris) Murray (deceased).

Since all the recipients were in agreement that all of the slaves were to be freed, it mattered not that the allotments would have divided some of the slave families.

By 1844, according to their father's wishes, each of James Cheston's children manumitted all of their allotted slaves.

"This was the form to be used when granting complete freedom to a slave that the Anne (Cheston) Morris and Dr. Caspar Morris had legally held in bandage at Ivy Neck Farm, Anne Arundel County, MD.

"FORM OF MANUMISSION"

"To All whom it may Concern be it known that I, ... of .... in the State of ...., for divers good causes & considerations, me thereunto moving, have released from Slavery, liberated, manumitted &

set free, and by these presents, do hereby release from Slavery, liberate, manumit & set free, my negroe man/woman, named .... being of the age of ...., also my negroes (&c as many as there may be), all on my farm in Anne Arundel County, State of Maryland, all able to work to gain a sufficient livelihood & maintenance, and the before named negroes, I do declare to be henceforth free, manumitted & discharged, from all manner of service or servitude to me, my executors or administrators forever.

In Witness whereof I have hereunto set my hand & seal this .... day of .... in the year of our Lord ...."

This was to be executed before two Witnesses in the presence of a Magistrate, with Anne & Caspar present, and in the presence of a commissioner (with same witnesses) appointed by the State of Md. to take testimony in Penna."

Richard Neal was part of the allotment which went to Anne (Cheston) Morris and her husband, Dr. Caspar Morris.

Richard Neal's Manumission Paper - 1843 [1e]

Richard Neal's manumission paper [1e] reads:

"MARYLAND,

Anne Arundel County. To wit

I, WILLIAM S. GREEN, Clerk of Anne ArundelCounty Court, do hereby certify, that it hath been provedto my satisfaction, that the Bearer hereof, named .... Richard ....Neal .... aged about ... thirty three .... years, ...about .. five .. feet .. eight and. a half .. inches high, .. brown ..complexion, has ... a ... scar ... on ... the ... forehead ... and .... another ... on ... the ... right ... cheek, ... is ... one .. of.. the .... persons ...... manumitted ...... by ...... Caspar ...... Morris .... and ... his ... wife, ... by ... deed ... dated ... the ... Sixth .... day .... of .... August, ... in .... the .... year .... Eighteen .... hundred .. and .. forty .. four, ...and that ... he .. was raised in the County aforesaid.

*(seal of
A . A . Co.)*

In Testimony Whereof, I hereto set my name, and affix the Seal of Anne Arundel County Court, this .. 10 .. day of .... November .... in the year of our Lord one

*thousand eight hundred and
forty .. four .....*

*(signed) Wm. S. Green,
A.A. Co t y. M d."*

Dr. Caspar Morris' sympathies were warmly
enlisted for the abolition of Negro slavery, yet
without carrying him into fanaticism which at
that time began to reign. The horrors of the slave
system, pushed as it was to the breeding for sale,
and the treatment of the poor sufferers, galled his
very soul and led him to exclaim the words of
William Cowper, his favorite poet:

*"I had much rather be myself the slave
and wear the bonds, than fasten them on him." [3]*

Dr. Caspar Morris at age 37 [3]
FROM A PAINTING BY REMBRANT PEALE

At the outbreak of the Civil War, all of Caspar Morris' sympathies were with the Union cause. Still, being of Quaker background, he very strongly resisted giving his son, Galloway, permission to enlist in the Union Army. Finally, after much discourse, in the end he writes [1a] :

".......... *If you can not stay without suffering more than I shall do, You must go. I would still implore you not to go. It seems impossible for me to submit. Do pray - withdraw.*"

Each one of the Cheston children set free the portion of slaves which came to him or her, and thus fulfilled the desire of their father, as well as carried out their principles on the subject.

In a letter in 1896 [2], Dr. Morris' son, Galloway Morris, writes to his nephew Lawrence J. Morris, recalling the release of the slaves. He writes that he distinctly remembers; "..... *the time when the announcement was made to the slaves, who had been called together for the purpose of making the announcement to them, that they were to be freed. All were freed who were young enough to come under the age* [age 45] *at which manumission was forbidden by the law of Maryland, and those who were too old* [older than 45] *were still to consider themselves as if they had been freed. They were, however, all told that they could remain in the employ of their several owners if they so desired, and most of them preferred to so remain.*

"Among those who elected to remain on their old places was Richard Neale."

Those who were under the age of legal manumission in the State of Maryland (21 years old) still had their freedom papers made out so that there was no question that they were free when they came of age.

Following the Cheston family sibling's release of their slaves there was much resentment and complaint about the Cheston "Free Niggers" because they were considered a bad influence on the slaves of the neighboring plantations. It was that they were enticing or helping other slaves to run away from their masters. Many of these neighboring owners sold those of their slaves who were married to any of the Cheston "Free Niggers". Several members of the Cheston family bought these slaves and allowed them to "work out" their costs, but they at once made out their manumission papers thus putting them on their honor to complete that obligation. There is no record of any one of them not doing so.

Commodore Mayo's feelings aligned with those of the other surrounding neighbors regarding the "Cheston Free Niggers" as being a bad influence, contaminating their slaves. However he would not sell Richard's wife or her children to any of the Cheston family.

Cheston free servants on steps at Ivy Neck

Chapter 5

ATTEMPT TO GATHER THE FAMILY

Richard struggled to save money enough to purchase his wife and family from Captain Mayo.

After being granted his freedom in 1844, Richard Neal continued to work on one of the Cheston farms for about a year.

He then attempted to make a living farming a 120 acre island, part of the Mayo Neck Plantation, which he leased from Captain Mayo, the master of his wife, Matilda, for $125.00 per year. Out of season, he helped a neighbor, Richard Carman clear land.

In his second affidavit of February 5th, 1853 [1c] sworn before Mayor Charles Gilpin of Philadelphia, Richard states: *".......... There was a house on it, but not fit to live in. The fences altogether out of repair; I made a new fence about 150 panels long and 10 rails high. I stocked the farm myself; I bought 3 horses, ploughs, hoes, a corn harrow, and a wagon; the forks and rakes I made myself. I bought harness and everything necessary for farming, except a clod harrow which Capt. lent me once. The stock, cow, pigs and horses, I furnish myself.*

I barrowed a cart of the Capt. twice to haul logs. A man and myself spent winter mauling rails; they were left on the farm and used for fencing, for which no allowance was made me. The Capt. found clover seed and plaster. It was a sandy Island and in bad order; Fences very bad when I went on it. I gathered sea grass and ploughed it in to enrich the land. I had it not quite four years; I paid rent for 3-3/4 years by checks on my agent in Baltimore. I had about $300.00 when I began; When I sold off I had about $500.00. I worked very hard while there and not clearing anything by the farm, gave it up. The Capt. said you are giving it up just when you are going to make something. I told him I had to pay high wages and the farm would not afford it and I was just paying away what I made other ways. While I was farming for Capt. Mayo, I followed huckstering generally through the neighboring and sometimes in Baltimore. I made a good deal by it and by catching oysters I often made ten to twenty dollars a week, and sometimes more than thirty. I could not have paid the hands on the farm if it had not been for that. I sold a great many opened oysters by the gallon, through the neighborhood. After I had put the farm in order it was rented for $100.00. The Capt. had to put the house in order before Mr. Young, the new tenant, would take it. He promised to do the same for me but never did it. The house was so open that my men would not stay and people would come and steal my chickens and turkeys while they were away. I gave up the farm in the fall and went to chopping wood for Capt. Dawson and took my victuals from home and did not board at Capt. Mayo's. I often furnished my family, who *were servants of Capt. Mayo, with flour, tea, coffee, and sugar; sometimes clothes and other articles. When I ate at my wife's quarters it was out of my own provisions and not Capt. Mayo's".*

Chapter 6

IMPATIENCE & VENGEANCE

Richard Neal's wife, Matilda grew impatient, and in the fall of 1849, along with seven other slaves, she ran away with her 5 children. They made their way to Baltimore by water.

Matilda's affidavit of Feb. 5th, 1853 [1c] continues "........ *I came away with a gang of slaves from the neighborhood; there were seven head besides myself and children. I had not seem Richard for three weeks, and did not see him till I came to Philadelphia after being purchased by the Cheston family. He did not in any way assist or encourage me to run away. I was in Baltimore four days before I was arrested, and never saw nor heard of Richard while I was there. I was in prison two weeks. I was sold to a trader from Tennessee of the name of Gordon with all my children. Captain Mayo told him to take us out of the State as far as "Wind and water would carry us". He told him he wished him to separate us "Three thousand miles apart". This was in my presence. The Captain told me my babe was to be sold from my breast. Mr. Gordon told me afterward that we were not to be sold together but each one to a different person. It was Capt. Mayo's request. My babe was about a year old and he told me my babe was to be sold from me.*

"Mr. Gordon told me to keep in good heart and we should all go together. A gentleman followed us out of Baltimore six miles, and bought me and my baby. Mr. Gordon took the children to Richmond. Mr. Pollion there bought the rest of the children as I understood. ......"

Quoting from part of Richard Neal's second affidavit of Feb. 5th, 1853 [1c], he states *"....... When my wife made her escape the family were living at Elk Ridge 10 or 15 miles from Baltimore. I was in Baltimore and saw in the papers that she had runaway. I had taken up marketing chickens and some apples.*

"Expecting the Capt. would blame me for it, I went to Philadelphia to see Dr. Morris . This was in the fall of 1849. I never advised her to run away, nor did I assist her in doing it. I did not give her any money. What she had she must have taken out of my trunk, as she had the key.

"When I was in Baltimore at the time my wife ran away, I did not see her. I heard some one say that a colored woman and children were taken down in Pratt Street by an officer; from the description I thought it must be her. When she spoke of running away, I told her not to do it but to conduct herself well and she need not fear nobody disturbed me. This was when she complained of being ill used and was threatened to be sold. The Capt. had sold two women a few weeks before; a daughter and mother. I never threatened my wife to take away her children, nor any way encouraged her to think of going off; but

always advised against it. I told her if she did run away she would be caught and whipped as others had been. She said she would just as leave be in Georgia, and she would not have staid 3 years after she was married if it had not been for me.

"When I saw in the newspapers that she had run away, I did not know which way she had gone, and I did not know she was in Baltimore till I heard that a woman like her and the children had been taken up. I have never been back to Maryland since I first came to Philadelphia to see Dr. Morris. Feeling afraid the woman and children were mine I got a person to look in the newspaper; he found the advertisement, read it and showed it to me. I saved $500.00 and have saved with my family since I came to Philadelphia $300.00 more. I have paid back part of what was subscribed to help me pay for my wife and children. I have been living with Mr. Sharpless steadily for about 2 years and 8 months and worked for him before, back and forth, for several months. It is 3 years and 3 months since I came to Philadelphia, and I have never been in Maryland since."

Sworn and subscribed Feb. 5th   (signed)
                               Richard Neal

1853 before me

(signed) *Charles Gilpin - Mayor"*

When Richard came North to Philadelphia, he went to Dr. Morris for help. Dr. Morris helped Richard to find work with the Sharpless family as an ostler (a stable hand/coachman) during this time. Mr. Townsend Sharpless was a leading Dry Goods Dealer, a Quaker, and a rather prominent Anti-Slavery proponent. The Sharpless family lived on Arch Street and had a stable on Cherry Street near Sixth Street.[12]

Richard's hope was to raise enough money to purchase his family's freedom. Through Dr. Morris, Mr. Sharpless, and appeals to other leading citizens and abolition groups, along with his own labors and savings, he was able to raise $3,268.

An effort was made to buy the family in Baltimore by a leading Quaker, Mr. Francis King, but it was found that the slave dealer who had purchased the family from Capt. Mayo, a Mr. Gordon, had made a special bargain by which he was bound not to sell anyone of this family in the State of Maryland, and also not to sell any two of them to the same person. Also, he was further bound not to sell any two of them in the same state.

Mr. King followed Mr. Gordon with his "Lot" of slaves, including Matilda and the children, and when the train crossed out of Maryland at Harpers Ferry, the dealer broke his bargain with Capt. Mayo, and Mr. King was able to purchase both the mother and her youngest child, a babe in arms. Another child was purchased at Richmond, but the last of them could not be bought until the "Lot" reached Mobile. The greater part of the family was gathered together in Savannah and came to Philadelphia by steamer from there.

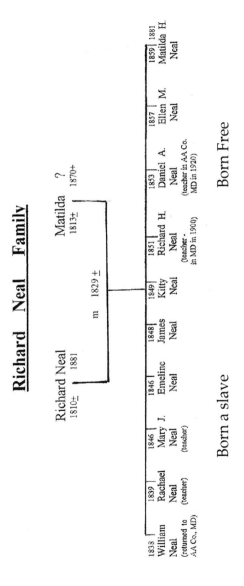

Richard Neal Family

Richard Neal
1810± 1881

Matilda ?
1813± 1870+

m 1829±

Born a slave

1838	1839	1846	1846	1848
William Neal (returned to AA Co., MD)	Rachael Neal (teacher)	Mary J. Neal (teacher)	Emeline Neal	James Neal

Born Free

1849	1851	1853	1857	1859	1881
Kitty Neal	Richard H. Neal (teacher - in MD in 1900)	Daniel A. Neal (teacher in AA Co. MD in 1920)	Ellen M. Neal	Matilda H. Neal	

Chapter 7

TOGETHER AND FREE
❧

Matilda's affidavit [1c] continues: "………
*The person who purchased me sent me on to
Philadelphia the same day; where I was manumitted by
Mrs. Morris, wife of Dr. Morris. The Children did not
come on for some weeks, waiting till the money could
be raised, as I understood. The money I brought away
with me I took from my trunk. It was Richards's money,
he always left it in my care, I kept the key of the trunk.
When my master asked me in the prison yard why I ran
away, I said nothing. Then he said, what do you think I
ought to do, sell you or take you home? I said "Sell me,
Sir". Matilda, he said, "Girl, I am sorry for you, to see
you such a dammed fool. Your Mistress says bring you
home"; but he said "I am afraid to do it." I told him I
had not wished to go, I would rather be sold; after this
he said good-bye and gave me half a dollar.*

*I never told Capt. Mayo that "It was Richards doing",
I never told Capt. Mayo that "Richard threatened to
take my children from me".*

*I never told him, nor thought of saying that "I can
never look my mistress in the face". I never told him
that "Free or slave I would not get such a home"."*

Following their reunion, Richard, Matilda and their family appear to have lived quiet, respectable and industrious lives, Richard as a coachman for Townsend Sharpless, Matilda as a washerwoman, and the children attending school. The Neals had a house in a street running west from 12th Street between Walnut and Locust Streets in Philadelphia.

CHAPTER 8

RENEWED VENGEANCE

It appears that Mayo's vengeance festered for more than 3 years before it finally boiled over in January of 1853.

Commodore Mayo, on the strength of the oath of one of his own slaves, went to Governor Lowe of Maryland and requested the Governor to submit a requisition upon the Governor of Pennsylvania for the extradition of Richard Neal to Maryland to stand trial for enticing his wife and family to run away.

Sworn and certified affidavits were taken from Commodore Mayo and his slave, William Hunter. On the strength of these affidavits, Governor Lowe issued a requisition to Governor Bigler of Pennsylvania for the arrest and extradition of Neal to Maryland.

Slave William Hunter's Sworn Affidavit [1a]

"State of Maryland,

Anne Arundel County, to wit:

"Be it remembered on this 20th. day of January 1853, personally appeared negro William Hunter, slave of Commodore Isaac Mayo, U.S.N. before me the subscriber, a Justice of the Peace for the County and State aforesaid, and makes oath on the Holy Evangely of Almighty God that he the said William Hunter was in the kitchen at Commodore Isaac Mayo's farm on Elkridge, in Howard County of this State, one night some time in the fall of 1849, on or about four o'clock in the morning, two black men, and one white man came there, one of the black men Richard Neal a free black man did then and there entice and persuade the following named slaves to run away, viz: Matilda Neal, Rachael Neal, Emeline Neal, James Neal and a child named Catherine Neal, children of Matilda Neal, and further that said Richard Neal did bundle up said slaves clothes and they all left in company with Richard Neal.

"Sworn before,   J. W. Hunter"

(James W. Hunter, Esq., Justice of the Peace)

Commodore Mayo's Sworn Affidavit [1a]

"State of Maryland,

Anne Arundel County, to wit:

  "Be it remembered on this 20th day of January 1853, personally appeared Com. Isaac Mayo of the U.S.N. before me a Justice of the Peace for the County and State aforesaid, and makes oath on the Holy Evangely of Almighty God, that the parties mentioned in the aforegoing affidavit of William Hunter charging Richard Neal with enticing and persuading his slaves to run away were owned and possessed by him when said slaves were enticed and persuaded to run away from him by said Richard Neal, and that said Richard Neal is a fugitive from Justice of this State, and believes he has taken refuge in the State of Pennsylvania.

  "Sworn before,   *J. W. Hunter."*

Certification of the Affidavits [1a]

"State of Maryland

Anne Arundel County, to wit:

  "I hereby certify that James W. Hunter, Esq., before whom the aforegoing affidavits were made and who has therefore subscribed his name was at the time of so doing a Justice of the Peace of the State in and for said County, duly commissioned & qualified.

*IN TESTIMONY WHEREOF I here
to set my hand and affix the seal
of the Circuit Court for Anne
Arundel County this 20th day
of January 1853. N. H. Green,
C'l'k C. C. for A. A. County*

The Requisition [1a]

"STATE OF MARYLAND

To wit:

*ENOCH LOUIS LOWE, Governor of the State
of Maryland,*

*To His Excellency, the Governor
of Pennsylvania.*

*"IT APPEARS BY THE ANNEXED PAPERS, duly
authenticated according to the laws of this State, that
Richard Neal (negro) stands charged upon the affidavit
of William Hunter (negro) with the crime of enticing
and persuading a certain Matilda Neal, Rachael Neal,
Emeline Neal, James Neal and a child named Catherine
Neal, the slaves of a certain Isaac Mayo to run away
from their Master against the form of the Act of the
General Assembly of Maryland in such case made and
provided, and it has been represented to me that he has
fled from the justice of this State, and has taken refuge
within the State of Pennsylvania.*

"NOW THEREFORE, Pursuant to the provision of the Constitution and Laws of the United States in such cases made and provided, I do hereby request that the said

(Seal)   RICHARD NEAL

be apprehended and delivered to

JOHN LAMB

who is hereby duly authorized to receive and convey to the State of Maryland, here to be dealt with according to law,

(SEAL)
"IN WITNESS WHEREOF, I have hereunto affixed my name, and the Great Seal of the State, this twenty-first day of January in the year of our Lord one thousand eight hundred and fifty three.

E. Louis Lowe

BY THE GOVERNOR

Thos. H. O'Neale

Secretary of State."

Gov. Bigler's warrant for the arrest of Richard Neal [1a]

"PENNSYLVANIA, ss,

(Great Seal)   *In the Name and by Authority of the Commonwealth of Pennsylvania*

WILLIAM BIGLER
Governor of the said Commonwealth

"To Hon. Oswald Thompson, President Judge of the 1st Judicial District or any other Judge, Alderman or Justice of the Peace in this Commonwealth,

"SENDS GREETINGS

"WHEREAS, It is provided and declared in, and by the second section of the fourth article of the Constitution of the United States, 'That a person charged in any State with treason, felony, or other crime, who shall flee from justice, and be found in another State, shall, on demand of the Executive authority of the State from which he fled, be delivered up, to be removed to the State having jurisdiction of his crime.' *

AND WHEREAS, his excellency, E. Louis Lowe, Governor of the State of Maryland, has given information to me that, a certain

RICHARD NEAL (negro)

stands charged on oath of William Hunter, duly made before James W. Hunter, a Justice of the peace in and for the County of Anne Arundel in the State of Maryland, with the crime of enticing and persuading a certain Matilda Neal, Rachael Neal, Emeline Neal, and a child named Catherine Neal, the slaves of a certain Isaac Mayo, to run away from their Master, committed in said County and State, and the said Governor has also requested that I would cause the said

RICHARD NEAL

to be apprehended, secured and delivered up to John Lamb, Agent on the part of the State of Maryland, as a fugitive from justice, to be removed for trial in the said State of Maryland having jurisdiction of his crime aforesaid, agreeable to the Constitution of the United States, and the provisions of an act of Congress, passed the twelfth day of February in the year one thousand seven hundred and ninety three:

"AND WHEREAS, the desire to punish the perpetration of crimes obnoxious to the order and happiness of society, as well as a due attention to the reciprocal obligations imposed upon the several States of the Union, in and by the said recited section of the Constitution, and the Laws of the United States, made in pursuance thereof, do require a prompt and diligent compliance with the said requisition of the Executive authority of the State of Maryland.

"THESE ARE, THEREFORE, to authorize and require you, the said Hon. Oswald Thompson, or any Judge, Alderman or Justice of the Peace in this Commonwealth as aforesaid, to issue a warrant in due form of law, directed to any constable, or other proper officer, for apprehending and securing the said Richard Neal and that when secured, you will cause him to be delivered up to John Lamb, Agent as afore said, to the intent that he may be removed from this State into the State of Maryland having jurisdiction of his crime; the said Agent peaceably and lawfully behaving.

"GIVEN under my hand and the Great Seal of the State, at Harrisburg, this twenty-forth day of

January in the year of our Lord one thousand eight hundred and fifty-three and of the Commonwealth the seventy-seventh.

BY THE GOVERNOR.   *E. S. Goodrich,*

                         Dep. Secretary of the Commonwealth

* The Constitution of the United States under Article IV - Section 2 states:

"The Citizens of each State shall be entitled to all Privileges and Immunities of Citizens in the several States.

"A Person charged in any State with Treason, Felony, or other crime, who shall flee from Justice, and be found in another State, shall on Demand of the executive Authority of the State from which he fled, be delivered up, to be removed to the State having Jurisdiction of the Crime.

[No Person held to Service or Labour in one State, under the Laws thereof, escaping into another, shall, in Consequence of any Law or Regulation therein, be discharged from such Service or Labour, but shall be delivered up on Claim of the Party to whom such Service or Labour may be due.]" **

** Twelve years after the abduction and trial of Richard Neal this Article IV - Section 2 was changed by the Thirteenth Amendment, which was ratified on December 6, 1865, and currently reads:

"Amendment XIII

*"**Section 1.** Neither slavery nor involuntary servitude, except as a punishment for crime whereof the party shall have been duly convicted, shall exist within the United States, or any place subject to their jurisdiction.*
*"**Section 2.** Congress shall have the power to enforce this article by appropriate legislation."*

THE NEAL FAMILY AFFIDAVITS [1c]

In Richard Neal's first affidavit taken on February 5th, 1853, before Mayor Gilpin, he states:

"..... On Tuesday the 25th of January, 1853 about mid-day, I had been washing my carriage and gone out on a short errand. When I returned into Cherry Street to the stable of my employer, Mr. Townsend Sharpless, I saw Capt. Mayo and another man standing near the door of the carriage house. I crossed the street to our stable or coach-house door, near which they were standing. I had my hand in my pocket to take out my key, when the man standing by the Captain placed his hand on me and said he had a warrant for me and said I must go with him. I asked him what he was going to do with me?. He said he would let me know when he got down to the Court House. He then took me to Fifth St. and down to the Court House. The judge not being there, they said, they took me down to the Station House below Walnut (Street).

"On our way down Fifth Street, Captain Mayo came up and said he only wanted me for a witness against John Davis for bringing my son, Billy, up from the country. I said I knew nothing about John Davis, nor who brought Billy up, nor his Mother.

"Coming down the street I told him (the officer) I wanted him to let Mr. Sharpless and Dr, Morris know that they had taken me up for some cause, I did not know what. He said Mr. Sharpless did know.

"About the time we came to Fifth Street, Captain Mayo and another officer joined us, the Captain behind. I was about an hour and a half at the Station House. While I was there I asked the officer to let Mr. Sharpless and Doctor Morris know. He said they would let them know, I need not be afraid. While I was at the Station House, the Captain told me he only wanted me as a witness against John Davis, and if I would tell him what I knew, he had the power to let me go. From there I was taken by officer Lamb from Annapolis, whom I knew, and another officer, one of our police with a badge (Capt. Mayo staid behind) down to an office in South Street below Spruce.

"The Alderman asked Lamb if he could prove something, I did not hear what, he said he would rather call Capt. Mayo in. He came in a few minutes. He then kissed the Book. The Alderman then asked him whether I was the man; he said yes. The Alderman asked Capt. Mayo if I was free. The Captain said 'yes, ar'nt you Richard?'. I said 'you know whether I am free or not, and you need not ask me that!'. The papers were then given to one of them and we walked out to the pavement. ....."

Chapter 9

RUSH FOR THE LINE

Richard Neal's first affidavit [1c] continues: ".....
*There was a carriage there with the door open. I
asked where they were going now; the city police officer
said to the judge's, and I took hold of the post at the
door to prevent them pulling me into the carriage, and
said I thought you were going to let Mr. Sharpless and
Dr. Morris know. They said some person was gone to
let them know. Capt. Mayo said 'Hurry, Hurry, that
the way to do business, always hurry'. They pulled and
pushed me into the carriage and said they were going
to the judge's. Three police officers got into the carriage
with me........."* (officers Lamb, Tapper and Briest).

It seems that Captains Mayo made a costly mistake
at this point. In his vengeance, it appeared he took
the time to detour to the Neal family home, while
the rest of his party headed for the Philadelphia,
Wilmington and Baltimore train station.

Philadelphia, Wilmington, and Baltimore Rail Road Station, Philadelphia, Pennsylvania,

In his affidavit, <u>William</u> Neal [1c], age about fifteen years, oldest son of Richard and Matilda Neal of Philadelphia, states:

"I was formerly a slave of Captain Mayo near Annapolis, Maryland. On the afternoon of Tuesday 25th of January, 1853 my Father and Mother were away from home. I was sitting at the table, near the window, with the other children, when Capt. Mayo knocked. I saw him and knew him; I then put on my hat and started after mother. When I got to the alley I saw the Capt. and he asked me, how did I do. He walked up to me, but I walked away from him. He said he would call and see mother. Before I left the house I heard him say that father was half way to Maryland before this time, and he said 'You will never see him again'. When I got to the corner of 12th Street there was a carriage there. The driver beckoned me to come to him, but I went away. As I came out of the alley along side of our house I saw the Captain peeping up the alley. I passed close by as I went

out. I told him I was going to see mother and asked him to wait awhile. There was no one in the carriage. I looked in thinking father might be there. I watched the carriage after the Capt. got into it; They drove up Locust Street.

"When in Baltimore Prison with my mother I was taken away and carried to Annapolis and put in prison there. When at Annapolis they asked me who took me to Baltimore and whether Father did it; I told them, No. They then asked me who did it; I told them I did not Know. They asked me if I did not go to Baltimore by water. I told them, Yes Sir!"

In the last of the five affidavits given by the Neal family on February 5th, 1853, <u>Rachel</u> Neal [1c], the oldest daughter age about fourteen, says: *"My mother and children were slaves of Captain Mayo in Maryland. On Tuesday 25th of January 1853 after dinner time in the afternoon several of us children were at home, Father and mother were away. There was a knock at the front door, I raised the window. The shutters were pulled open by someone outside, I then saw Capt. Mayo there. The Captain asked me where my mother was. He asked me if I knew he had father. I made no answer. He asked me again the same question. I them said, No Sir. He then said he had him and expected he was now half way to Maryland. My younger sister, Mary, went out after mother. As she passed by him, he asked her if she knew him and then said if she had stayed with him she would not have had smallpox, and that her beauty was gone. He then told me that he would come and see mother and if she would do what he wanted her to do he would let father come back."*

Because Captain Mayo has detoured to the Neal home to vent his wrath on Matilda and the children, he also misses the train south. At the station, he found the rest of his party had proceeded south in the carriage without him.

Richard Neal's affidavit continues: *"...... They went to the Baltimore Depot. Before we got there, I said 'I thought you were going to the judge's'. Then they said 'We are going down to Baltimore with you. Captain Mayo only wants you for a witness against John Davis.' The (train) cars were gone, they said at the depot, about two minutes. The carriage then crossed at the Market Street Bridge and went on to Chester where we arrived about six or seven o'clock."*

"When taken from home, I was preparing the carriage to take Mrs. Sharpless to The House of Refuge, she was one of the ladies committee and visited the house once a week; calling in the carriage for several other persons, which I had been in the practice of doing for several weeks of a Tuesday. I had no chance of letting her know that I had been taken away."

Near Darby, PA, when they stopped to water the horses, Richard bolted from the coach and started running. A two-mile chase ensued and Richard was finally recaptured and roughed up before returning to the carriage, and they continued on towards Chester.

Richard's affidavit continues: "...... *When I was caught after I escaped from the carriage near Darby, and had given my self up and was sitting on a log, one of the officers struck me on the bare head with his Billy. It stunned me and made me light headed, and I could not get up for a little while. He was one of the City police. He was the one that told me that they had sent word to Mr. Sharpless and Dr. Morris. ....".*

Meanwhile Galloway Cheston Morris, the youngest son of Dr. Caspar Morris, was at home sick that day when one of the older of the Neal children came knocking frantically at Dr. Morris' door in great excitement to say that Commodore Mayo had stopped at the house to see their mother. Matilda was away at work. Captain Mayo told the children to tell their mother that "he had their father and they would never see him again".

Young Galloway immediately went to find his father, and the two of them then went to the Station house on 15th Street below Walnut where they found there had been an arrest of a "fugitive slave", he had been hurried off to the depot at Broad and Prime (now Washington Ave.) - the old Philadelphia, Wilmington & Baltimore R.R. station. At the station they determined that Mayo's party had missed the train and started south in a carriage.

Chapter 10

DELAY AT CHESTER

Mayo's party arrived in Chester around six o'clock, and proceeded to the Goff Hotel (commonly known as The Steamboat Hotel) at the bottom of Market Street on the river front, where they took a private dinning room for dinner. A servant, while waiting on the party, overheard that Richard was an accused fugitive who was being hurried south. The servant took this news out into the town and soon, a large mixed crowd of blacks and white abolitionists began to gather.

Goff Hotel - Chester, PA [8]

Meanwhile, back in Philadelphia, young Galloway Morris went to Richard's home and secured Richard's manumission paper, which Richard no longer had to carry with him in the northern free state of Pennsylvania. With this proof that Richard is a free man, his father, Dr. Morris, and Mr. Sharpless sought out lawyer friends and associates, including the well known legal writer and educationalist, Francis Wharton, along with the former mayor of Philadelphia, Peter Mc Call, and Dr. Morris's lawyer cousin, Pemberton Morris. They obtained a writ of habeas corpus from Judge Thompson of the Philadelphia Court of Quarter Sessions.

Armed with the writ, Dr. Morris's eldest son, James Cheston Morris, along with two of the city police officers and several anti-slavery oriented acquaintances, start south towards Baltimore on the evening train to try to stop Richard's abduction. They knew only that Mayo's party was headed south for the Mason-Dixon Line in a carriage. They thought that due to the snow that was starting to fall rather heavily, Mayo's party might try to get Richard onto the south bound train at some station further south.

When they reached Chester, low and behold, they are met by Richard and his captors attempting to board the train to continue south towards Wilmington and Baltimore.

P.W.B. RR Station - Chester, PA [8]

Richard's first affidavit continues;

"...... *In the evening, when the cars from Philadelphia arrived at Chester, they had me at the Depot. Captain Mayo met us at the door. He told them (the officers);* '*Come on, come on, hurry on*'. *Captain Mayo took hold of me.* '*I had hand cuffs on.*' *The captain said I should go. The crowd prevented my being forced in, and the cars started without us.* ......"

Richard had physically become the "rope" in a tug-of-war between the Maryland abductors and the Pennsylvania abolitionist on the station platform at Chester. The proslavery group was the stronger of the two parties, and would have probably succeeded but for one old gentleman, a strong antislavery but non-violent man, Thomas Garrett of Wilmington. Mr. Garrett was at the top of the steps on the platform of the train car into which one of the officers of Mayo's party was endeavoring to drag Richard feet first. Without a smile on his face old Mr. Garrett reached down and took the officer by the ankles from behind and picked them up thus propelling the officer face down and head first into the crowd below.

Train car steps [1]

The train conductor, Mr. Boucher, held the train for more than ten minutes beyond its' scheduled stop time and he became anxious that his schedule was being delayed. He signaled his engineer to proceed. The train departed leaving both parties standing on the station platform.

There is a stand off. The northern party produced the writ of habeas corpus from the Philadelphia court. Mayo's party claimed Chester was out of

Philadelphia's jurisdiction and the Governor's warrant for arrest took precedent. Mayo's party appeared to have the legal upper hand. If they would have driven with him the few miles further south to the Delaware line, it would have become much more difficult to recover him. Due to the ire of some of the crowd, and the snow storm in progress, Mayo's party decided to take Richard back to the Chester jail house for the night.

Chester City Court House [1]

Richard was held over night, Tuesday, January 25th, in the Chester City jail. The intent of Mayo's party was to catch the first train south in the morning:

"...... When I was in Chester, I was locked in prison. I was handcuffed and chained to the floor. Captain Mayo staid in the room all night to watch. The officers came in once in a while. Two other prisoners were in the same room. Captain Mayo had a bottle of brandy in the room,

and I saw him drink frequently of it during the night. There was a second bottle brought in. I was offered it but would not drink. They talked of taking me away in the night in a carriage, and said about mid-night the people would be gone. Billy Green called the Captain to the window and said there were 50 or 60 people about the house, niggers among them. The Captain slept part of the night, leaning on a stepladder, part of it on a settee. The Captain never told me what the true charge was against me, but always said it was to be a witness against John Davis, and said if I would tell him what I knew he would let me go. When in the Alderman's office (in Philadelphia) *no charge was made against me that I heard. He did not read anything to me. He only asked me if I had anything to say. I said, No, but turned around and said to the men 'I thought you were going to send for Mr. Sharpless and Dr. Morris'. While in Chester, Capt. Mayo told a man that I had taken off about $15,000 worth of slaves from him within two years; he was going away and was afraid I would take off the remainder. That he had given me a first rate farm for mere nothing, and I made two or three thousand dollars on it and that was the way I treated him."*

Sworn & Subscribed, Feb. 5th, 1853   (signed)
Richard Neal.

      Before me,

(signed) Charles Gilpin. Mayor."

At this point, the party trying to save Richard Neal returned to Philadelphia with the intent to rectify the jurisdictional issue. They got the lawyer and former Mayor, Peter McCall, out of bed. In consultation, he advised them to attempt to get a writ of Habeas Corpus from the Supreme Court of the State of Pennsylvania which was meeting the next day in Philadelphia. They proceeded to the home of the Clerk of Prothonotary and, getting him out of bed, they all went to the Merchants Hotel, at 4th above Arch Street at which several of the Supreme Court Judges were staying.

With a writ of Habeas Corpus they obtained from the Supreme Court of Pennsylvania in hand, they returned to Chester on the first train in the morning.

In the meantime they sent Dr. Morris's eldest son, J. Cheston Morris, to Governor Bigler in Harrisburg with three letters. Two of the letters were basically letters of introduction. The first letter was from lawyer, Francis R. Wharton, and the second letter was from Neal's employer, Townsend Sharpless. The third letter was from Dr. Morris, to explain the conditions of the case as he knew them, and to request a stay against the Executive warrant on Richard Neal.

Lawyer Francis Wharton's letter [11]

"My dear Sir:-

"Mr. Morris who bears this letter is the son of Dr. Caspar Morris, a gentleman of the highest weight in this city. His object is to ask a stay of proceedings on an

Executive warrant for the arrest of a man named Richard Neal. I can only say that if the facts he offers to prove are true, viz: that Neal was not a resident of Maryland at the time of committing the alleged crime, - the case seems within the rule laid down by Mr. Kane, and adopted by Gov. Shunk, (see 6 Pa. La. J. 418) to which I particularly invite your attention. The hardships are many, and will be stated by Mr. Morris.

Truly yours,

Jan. 26, 1853.   *Francis Wharton.*

Employer Townsend Sharpless' letter [11]

"Philad. 1/25th, 1853

"To Governor Bigler

"Respected Friend

"It was my intention to have accompanied my young friend, son of Dr. Morris, to Harrisburg, with a view to induce thy favorable consideration of the Case of Richard Neal, but I am informed that my presence in Court in the morning, will be of importance.

"Richard had been in my employ <u>continuously</u>, I think for two years and eight months; and I am satisfied he could not have been in Maryland during that time. He was also employed occasionally for some months previous, by me.

"In the fall of 1849, my attention was called to him by a Subscription paper or book presented to me for a contribution; which is now before me and is dated Nov

11th, 1849. It was prepared and signed by Dr. Caspar Morris, and is as follows:

"'Richard Neale is one of the Servants of the late James Cheston of West River MD. He was emancipated together with all who belonged to that Estate, about six years since. He is the son of a most worthy couple, and has always conducted himself in a manner, to deserve and secure the respect and confidence of his employ. His wife and six children all under twelve years of age, were the property of Capt. Mayo of the United States Navy. Under an apprehension, that they were about to be sold, and thus separated from him, and perhaps from each other, they made an attempt to abscond. They were betrayed, returned and sold to a Trader, with the stipulation, that they should be carried out of the state of Maryland, and no two of them sold to one person. The effort is now being made to redeem them, from this state of distress. From my personal knowledge of Richard Neale, & the circumstances of the case, I commend him as worthy of sympathy and aid of the Benevolent.'

(signed Caspar Morris MD)

"To this Subscription Richard's own name was appended for $500; which it appears he had saved from time he had been emancipated. Three hundred dollars was subscribed by his fellow Servants; and was the entire amount of their own savings.

"The total amount paid for his family was $3,235.63. Several Hundred dollars has been saved by Richard since the purchase, and paid over to those who advanced the amount. It will therefore be seen that he must have

been very economical in his expenditures, which I know to have been the case, altho receiving good wages.

"Dr. Morris' family speak in the most confident manner, of his not being South, since he first came to the City, in the early part of November (11th mo.) 1849. And I am quite certain, he could not have been there, since he came into my Employ.

"Thou will excuse the liberty I have taken in addressing thee in this behalf, in consideration of the desire to do an act of justice to a deserving man, and one who I believe is about to be oppressed.

"Respectfully thy friend

Townsend Sharpless"

Dr. Caspar Morris' letter [11]

"To His Excellency Gov. Bigler

"Dear Sir

"My friend Mr. Francis Wharton having done me the honor to introduce me to your notice I take the liberty of stating the facts in the case of Richard Neale as I am prepared to prove them in a Court of law.

"Richard was born the slave of my father in law James Cheston Esquire of Baltimore & Ann Arundel County Maryland and upon the death of said James Cheston was together with other servants and property awarded to my wife. He with some others was by me manumitted in the year 1844 as appears by the certificate of the clerk

of the Court of Ann Arundel County Maryland now in my possession. He had married a slave of Commodore Isaac Mayo, and immediately on receiving his own freedom set himself with all diligence and economy, in the employ of the said Commodore Mayo to laying up sufficient sum to purchase the freedom of his wife and children. For some cause to me unknown he fell under the displeasure of Commodore Mayo who threatened to sell his wife to a dealer in slaves, under the apprehension that this threat would be accomplished she contrary to the advice of her husband Richard attempted to escape from slavery with her children. They were arrested by an agent of Commodore Mayo & by him sold to a dealer in Negros with the stipulation that he should not sell them again in the state of Maryland. Under these circumstances Richard came to me in Philadelphia and soliciting my interference paid into my hands the sum of six hundred dollars which he had saved and with the aid of some of my friends we raised the large amount of Three thousand two hundred & odd dollars which was paid for the wife and children who were purchased in the state of Virginia and brought here in the fall of the year 1849. Since that time they have been living virtuously and have been industrious thriving people.

"Richard has been constantly in the employ of Townsend Sharpless Esq. one of our wealthiest citizens and has not been absent from his house long enough to

reach the state of Maryland during the last three years. Nor could he have reached West River where Commodore Mayo resides without a pass from myself which I have never given him. He is I am confident, innocent of any crime against the laws of the state of Maryland. I am not an advocate of the Abolition of Slavery & and never in any way participated in the movements which have disrupted the harmony between the states.

I am (not) now a slave holder. My son will present this letter & I crave of your excellency such ____ as shall prevent the carrying Richard Neal out of the state.

> *"With all respect, I have the honor to*
> *subscribe myself,*
> *Your obdt. servant*
> *Caspar Morris*

"No. 12 Cheston Square
Chestnut St. Philad.
Jan. 26th, 1853"

The result is that Governor Bigler was convinced that a great injustice has been attempted. Governor Lowe of Maryland had mistakenly asked for Richard Neal's arrest as a <u>fugitive slave</u>, and that, as such, his office had issued the warrant for Richard.

While not at once revoking his warrant, he sent his private Secretary to Philadelphia to ask the Supreme Court not to intervene. The Secretary remained in Philadelphia until after the case was decided should the revocation be needed, which it was not.

.... **As the trial progressed** ....

At this point the Pennsylvania Senate begins to question Governor Bigler's action in this case:

"IN SENATE

January 27, 1853

WHEREAS, It has been represented that one Richard Neal a resident of Pennsylvania was on yesterday the 26th day of January 1853, arrested in the city of Philadelphia on a charge of inciting slaves to escape from their owners in Maryland, that said arrest was made upon the authority of a Requisition from the Governor of Maryland, complied with by the Executive of Pennsylvania.

"THEREFORE - -

"RESOLVE, That the Governor be requested to communicate to the Senate copies of the indictment or affidavit and requisition produced before him in said case together with copies of the corre-spondence (if any) on the subject, and reasons for his compliance with the said requisition of the Executive of Maryland.

(Extract from the Journal, John W. Sullivan, clerk)"

Editor's note:

Related news paper articles

Keep in mind that the following are direct transcripts, word for word, from actual contemporary newspaper articles of the time, written by those who were there, at the time of the occurrences. Although conflicting, I feel they are more accurate than I can describe. They do not necessarily reflect my views, but the views of those who were there at the time, in 1853, nor do they all agree completely with each other in detail.

From the Philadelphia *"Eve. Bulletin - Jan. 26th (?), 1853"*: [1d]

"CITY ITEMS"

"Arrest of an Alleged Fugitive From Justice -

"On Tuesday, a colored man by the name of Richard Neal, a manumitted slave, for some time past employed as ostler by Townsend Sharpless, was arrested on a requisition, upon the alleged charge of enticing away certain slaves from the estate of Commodore Isaac Mayo, of the United States Navy, in Anne Arundel, Maryland. The arrest was made by an officer from that State (John Lamb), *aided by two officers of this city.*

"The prisoner was brought before Alderman Kenney, and was, by that magistrate, committed to the custody of the Maryland officer, on his identity being established. The officer having him in charge, with the complainant, Commodore Mayo, thereupon determined upon the summary course of carrying him away from

Philadelphia, without allowing him to communicate with either his employer, family, or friends, inasmuch as they were fearful that they be delayed by some counter legal proceeding.

"They accordingly hastened to the Baltimore Depot, but were left by the two o'clock train. The officers then proceeded to Chester in a chaise. In the vicinity of Darby the negro suddenly jumped out of the window of the vehicle, and fled. He was chased through woods, over meadows and across fields, for some two miles, and was finally re-taken on Mr. Eastwick's place, in Kingsessing, with the aid of one of his men.

"At Chester, the officers waited for the 10 o'clock line. In attempting to put the prisoner aboard the cars, they were obstructed by a number of persons who had come down from the city with a writ of "habeas corpus" from Judge Thompson, of the Court of quarter Sessions. Being beyond the jurisdiction of the justice who had issued it, they disregarded the writ. A mob of blacks beset the cars, and while the officers were struggling to get the prisoner in, and his friends were trying to pull him back, the train started, leaving the whole party behind.

"The prisoner was taken to the Chester lockup, which was surrounded all night by a large mob of negroes, who were however, restrained from violence by the police and law-loving citizens of the town.

"When the eight o'clock train came down yesterday morning, (Wednesday, January 26th .... ed.) *the prisoner was brought out of confinement, and again taken to the cars, arrangements having been made to prevent a rescue. Just as the party, though, were entering one*

car, an officer came out of another with a writ of 'habeas corpus' from Justice Lowrie, of The Supreme Court (of Pennsylvania .... ed.). This stopped the progress, and Neal returned in the upward train. The writ will be heard today (Thursday, January 27th .... ed.)".

From Philadelphia "Eve. Bulletin - Jan. 27th 1853" (Thursday): [1d]

"The Case of the Negro Neal"

"Mr. Editor – In justice to Com. Mayo, it is hoped you will insert this in your very valuable paper, which, of yesterday has made a statement of the arrest, of the colored man, Richard Neal. The statement contained some inaccuracies.

Some fifteen or sixteen years ago, Neal married the women in the family of Commodore Mayo, named Matilda, who was then a valuable servant.

On Neal's becoming free, Commodore M. rented him a farm of 120 acres of highly improved land, at a very small rent, and furnished him, almost entirely, with the means of cultivating the same. Neal carried on the farm for several years, accumulated a valuable stock, and has cleared several thousand dollars.

All of a sudden Neal informed the proprietor that he must give up the farm, as it confined him too much. The Proprietor said 'Dick, you intend to play me some dirty trick', when he fell on his knees and called the Almighty to witness that he had no such intension. On being asked what intension, he said 'Master, you think that I intend to run away with Matilda and the children,' (of which the Commodore's confidential servants [William Hunter ... ed.] *had informed him). Neal sold off his crop and stock, and took up his abode in his wife's quarter near the great house. where he lived for several months, receiving his meals when there with the house servants. In July, the Commodore's family visited another of his estates* ["Blandair" at Elk Ridge, Maryland .... ed.] *forty miles distant, taking Matilda and all her children with them. In a few days the Commodore returned to his Bay Shore Estate, taking Billy, Matilda's eldest son, to drive the buggy. On the following morning the manager reported Billy not to be found, saying, at the same time, that he had threatened to whip him for not cleaning and feeding his horse. We took it for granted that he had gone to the upper farm. In the afternoon two gentlemen rode up and informed that Neal had the night before run away with Matilda and five of her children.*

The Baltimore police officers soon caught Matilda and all six of her children. Billy had been carried to Baltimore, as his mother stated, by John Davis, the relation of Neal; D. having stolen a boat and took Billy up by water. When the fugitives were apprehended, Neal escaped out the back door, as the officers entered the front. Conveyances were ready, and in a few moments more they would all have been off. With the reward of $500.00, and officers fees, their apprehension cost over $700.00.

"When Matilda was asked by her master what induced her to run away, she said it was all Richard's doings; that he had at her to go ever since he gave up the farm which she refused, and it was not until he said that he

would take the children and leave her that she consented to go. When asked what was to be done with her, she said sell me, master, for I can never again look my mistress in the face; remarking at the same time, free or slave, that she would never get such a home. They were all sold in Baltimore with express understanding that they were all to be kept together. Neal informed Com. M. but yesterday, that he had gone South and bought them with his own money. They are free and in Philada. As to his requesting to purchase his family it is utterly untrue. No proposition was ever made, or it would have been gladly acceded to. A short time before Neal took Matilda away, the confidential servants informed Com. Mayo that Neal had assisted John Davis, his relation, (another of the Cheston freed negroes) in taking away eight of the Commodore's most valuable servants; they have never been recovered. As to Neal's never having returned to Maryland, how can Mr. Sharpless know? for Neal lived at other places before he went into his employ, and the word of the Commodore's servants is as good as that of Mr. Sharpless.

"It was but the other day that another of the Cheston freed negroes was taken up for endeavoring to entice his wife away. The servant who testified to Neal's taking away his wife, (and upon which the Governor of Maryland made requisition upon the Governor of Pennsylvania), when asked by his master why he did not give the alarm, stated that a white man and two black men were along, all armed, and who kept watch whilst Neal packed up all the clothing, &c., of Matilda and the children, and says that he was sure, if he had

made any move, and his only escape was by the kitchen door, when he would pass within ten feet of the gang, that they would have killed him and also his mistress and the children. The manager's and other servants quarters, were some distant from the dwelling-house. There is no doubt but Matilda and her children will make a great flourish before the Court, to create sympathy – but is there no sympathy for the white man who is robbed of his property, with the probability of having his wife and children murdered?"

(unsigned)

From "True American, Trenton, Jan. 27th, 1853" (Thursday): [1d]

"FROM PHILADELPHIA"

(Correspondence of the True American)

Philadelphia, Jan. 26 - P.M.

"Terrible Doings in Negro-dom – Arrest of a Fugitive – His Escape and Recapture– Exciting Race – The Whig Abolitionist at Chester – Officers Mobbed and Assaulted – The Laws of Pennsylvania set at Defiance – Disgraceful Conduct – Where will it End, &c."

"On Tuesday morning, a colored man named Richard Neal, in the employ of Townsend Sharpless, was arrested by officer Trapper(Tapper), upon a requisition issued by Gov. Bigler, charging him with being a fugitive from

justice from the State of Maryland, in enticing away a number of slaves, the property of Capt. Mayo, U.S. Navy. The negro was taken before Ald. Kenny, and after a hearing, was remanded into the custody of Mr. John Lamb, of Annapolis, Agent of Capt. Mayo, who, with officer Tappen (Tapper) *and Briest, started for the two o'clock train for Baltimore. They arrived at the depot too late for the cars, but started in a cab for Wilmington. About two miles this side of Darby, the negro took advantage of the officers, and sprang from the cab. He took to the fields, through the woods and ditches, being closely pursued by the officers, Mr. Lamb, and the cad driver. After a chase over two miles, the match being nearly equal between Tappen and the darkey, the latter was captured, place again in the cab, and once the journey was recommenced.*

"About six o'clock, the party reached Goff's Hotel, Chester, ("The Steamboat Hotel" owned and managed by the Goff family .... ed.), *where they supped, having taken the precaution to secure a private room. Finding the load heavy, the horses fatigued, snow falling, and piercing cold, it was determined to proceed no farther, but take the cars at 9 o'clock for Baltimore. A colored servant at Goff's having caught sight of the prisoner, immediately sounded the alarm that Neal was a fugitive slave, and in a short time a large crowd of blacks had collected around the hotel. Officer Briest went out among then, and ascertained their object to be a rescue. He consulted with Mr. Lamb, and officer Tappen, as to the best course to pursue. Mr. B. went in pursuit of a magistrate, with the view of informing the*

blacks that the prisoner was no slave, but a free man, and a fugitive from justice from another State. After searching the town over, no magistrate could be found. Fortunately, police officer Isaiah Mirkle, – a gentlemanly, bold, fearless officer, – offered his valuable services, and with the gentlemen above named, the fugitive negro was taken from the hotel to the railroad depot, a distance of near half a mile, followed by a large crowd of blacks. No attempt at rescue was made. Had it been, there must have been a sacrifice of life on one side or the other. The parties having Neal in custody, were cool, resolute, and determined. Previous to the approach of the train, Y.S. Walters, the abolition proprietor of the 'Delaware County Republican' was shown the requisition from Gov. Bigler, with accompanying documents, and at once proclaimed them all satisfactory. The blacks took him at his word, and immediately dispersed. The train arrived just after eleven o'clock, and then commenced a scene of tumult and uproar. While the fugitive was being placed in the car, some half dozen ruffians sprang out, proclaiming they had a writ of 'habeas corpus', and Richard should not be placed in the car. Mr. Lamb stated that he held the prisoner upon a requisition from Gov. Bigler. The 'habeas corpus' was not read, neither was it believed to be genuine. The officer, who accompanied these gentlemanly ruffians, refused to act further in the premises, and they declined giving their names. Capt. Mayo, who was in the cars, hearing the noise, sprang out, when a terrible conflict took place, during which knives, pistols, and maces were drawn. The fugitive black was in the center of the melee. There were several persons on the platform of the car, and among them a person named Garrett, of Wilmington, who visits Philadelphia almost daily. Every time the fugitive would reach the platform, he would be pressed back by this fellow and his gang.

A tall young chap from Philadelphia, dressed in a white overcoat, held 'grim death' to the negro, and it was 'pull dick, pull devil' between the two opposing parties. After debating the case several minutes, the whistle sounded, and away they went, leaving the battle waging. Mr. Lamb, and the officers held on to Neal, and landed him in the lockup — a place just in keeping with the Whig abolitionists of Chester, who would embroil the whole American Union in civil war and bloodshed, merely for the sake of defending some worthless black rascal. During the entire night, the blacks hung about the lockup, many of them remaining until six o'clock this morning. Capt. Mayo, an honorable, noble hearted man, determined to remain with the fugitive until the early morning train arrived from Philadelphia, not withstanding he (the accused) could have been sent into Delaware in a very short time by means of horses, as there was nothing to prevent their departure from Chester. The very honorable young gentlemen, who came with their useless piece of paper, after creating a riot, assaulting the officers, sneaking back in the return train 'like kill sheep dogs', and have not since been seen or heard from. One Samuel Montgomery, who hails from God only knows where, did his utmost last night, at the depot, to create a breach of peace. He, however, soon hauled in his black colors.

"This morning, just before nine o'clock, the prisoner, in company with the officers, proceeded to the Railroad depot, followed by an immense mob of blacks and whites; and I am sorry to say many of the latter were ten times worse than the blacks and they were impudent enough. Mr. Walters, of the 'Republican' (newspaper), Sammy Smith, the big king among the Chester colored gentlemen, and Edward M. Farris, the little king, were busy for some hours previous, in drumming up their forces — but those having in custody Richard Neal were not to be intimidated. Upon arrival of the cars, the prisoner was conducted to the platform, and was met by Dr. Morris, his son, and a son of Townsend Sharpless, accompanied by a very nervous gentleman, who produced and read in a very trembling voice, a writ of 'habeas corpus' issued by the Supreme Court, commanding the release and appearance of Richard Neal before that august body. Mr. Lamb produced the Governor's requisition, and the next moment handed over the negro to the officer of the Court in question. A yell, such as you might hear among cannibals, was sent up and Richard Neal was released of his hand-cuffs, and re-conveyed back to the Chester lock-up. The conduct of the blacks was outrageous, and in the midst of the whole of it, not a few <u>black</u> white men acted a prominent part.

"One of the young gentlemen who accompanied Dr. Morris on his mission of mercy called at the Whig head quarters, and purchased poor Dicky Neal a good breakfast, which he had placed in a very neat little basket, and covered over with a clean sweet towel. The young man was very careful in the manner in which it was *carried to Richard, and Richard received it with heart-felt thanks.*

"But to conclude: Dr. Morris, the two young gentle-men, and poor Dicky Neal, obtained a private convey-ance, and proceeded forthwith to the city of Brotherly Love, where 'joy everlasting' awaited the unfortunate creature. Capt. Mayo came to the city in the same carriage. *

"Tuesday, (Thursday, January 27th.... ed.) at 12 o'clock, the case will be heard, and it then will be decided of what use is a Governor's requisition. Capt. Mayo has the services of Mr. L. Hirst as counsel."

* It was reported elsewhere that the Captain was so concerned for his safety, due to the high level of sentiment in Chester, that he begged to be allowed to return to Philadelphia with Dr. Morris's party. It was very cold that January day and while consenting to allow Captain Mayo to return with them, they made him take an outside seat on top of the carriage while Richard rode inside the carriage.

On Thursday, January 27, Richard was brought before The Supreme Court at the Court House on the south-east corner of 6th and Chestnut Street, in the North Room of the second floor. There was much excitement over the now widely publicized case and the court room was packed. Richard had initially been charged as a fugitive slave, when indeed he had never belonged to the Captain and, had been freed by Dr. & Mrs. Morris almost ten years prior.

When the issue was brought up before the court that the Governor of Maryland had made a mistake in using the form of requisition for a "Fugitive Slave" instead of that for a "Fugitive from Justice", the Supreme Court adjourned the case to allow them to prove that assertion. The assertion was disclaimed by Governor Lowe who stated that Commodore had himself applied for the requisition; that no mistake had been made, that the case did not concern the State of Maryland at all, and that there was no charge against Richard as a "Fugitive from Justice".

From the *"Chester County Republican* (Friday) *Jan. 28"* [1d]

"LOCAL INTELLIGENCE"

*"**Excitement** - - Considerable excitement was in this Borough (Chester) on Tuesday evening last, inconsequence of the arrival here of three men in a carriage, having with them a colored man who was shackled with handcuffs. The kidnapping of the Parker Girls, and the brutal murder of the unfortunate Miller by Maryland desperadoes, had aroused a feeling in this community against the action of the agents of slaveholders in surreptitiously conveying colored persons from among us, or through our town, and hence it was not long after the arrival of the party above alluded to, that inquiries*

began to be made as to the cause for which the man was detained. It appeared, from a requisition from Gov. Bigler, and certain papers from Alderman Kenney, of Philadelphia, in possession of one of the officers, that the man under arrest, whose name is Richard Neal, was charged with the <u>crime</u> of inciting <u>his own wife and children</u> to run away from a certain Captain Mayo, of Anne Arundel county, Md. The party who had the man in custody conveyed him to the rail road depot about nine o'clock, where a large number of persons had assembled, anxious to learn the charges against him. The requisition was shown by the officers - - all appeared fair - - the excitement passed off, and most of those present returned to their homes. The arrival of the down train brought Capt. Mayo, and just as the party were about to leave with their prisoner, an officer from the city, accompanied by two or three persons who knew the colored man, and were acquainted with the proceedings against him, made his appearance, and armed with a writ of ' <u>habeas corpus</u>', demanded that he should have a hearing before his departure for the South., An effort was made by the Southern gentlemen to get the colored man into the cars, but notwithstanding that the conductor, Mr. Boucher, <u>detained the train</u> some ten minutes longer than its usual stopping time, <u>there was not room for them</u>, and the cars finally left the party standing on the platform at the station. While the train was standing (apparently <u>waiting</u>) considerable crowding and pushing took place on the part of those who were anxious that the colored man should have fair play. The Marylanders flourished their pistols, and

*gave vent to their wrath in awful threats and impreca-
tions. A tall, gentlemanly looking man in a <u>white coat</u>,
held the habeas corpus, and coolly and collectedly defied
the slaveholder and his pistol. The colored man was
finally taken to the lock-up, where he remained guarded
until morning. Meanwhile, the timely aid which had
come from the city, left for home, carrying with them
their authority for detaining the alleged Prisoner, thus
putting the friends of justice here in doubt to what course
to pursue. Before the train from Philadelphia reached
here the next morning, several hundred citizens of this
Borough were assembled on the platform, awaiting the
course of events. There was no attempt at rescue (no
desire to interfere with the proper execution of the law),
but there was a determination to see it faithfully carried
out. The slaveholder and his posse, with their handcuffed man in charge, moved towards the cars, which
some thought, would soon convey the latter to a slave
prison in Maryland. Just as they were about entering
the cars, from which they were kept back a few moments
owing to the large crowd of persons in attendance,
an officer from the city appeared, and read a warrant
ordering the detention of Capt. Mayo and his party,
and requiring them to appear before the proper tribunal in Philadelphia, at a certain hour designated in the
writ. In vain did the old Captain flourish the document
obtained from Gov. Bigler, embellished with the big seal
of Pennsylvania, above the head of the officer - - he was
inexorable. The locomotive whistled - - the train started.
and a shout at the triumph of the law, went up which
made all ring again. The shackles were removed from*

the arms of the colored man, and, after a brief sojourn, he was taken to the city. Capt. Mayo went in the same conveyance, and the remainder of the party followed in the afternoon train.

"Since the above was written, we have received the Philadelphia papers, containing an account of the transaction, from which it appears that Neal had formerly been a slave in Maryland, but was manumitted by the family to which he belonged, and subsequently married a slave of Mayo's. After some time Neal removed to Philadelphia, and made an exertion to purchase his wife and children, but before he succeeded in his effort, the wife ran away with her children, and reached Baltimore, where the fugitives were recaptured, and there sold to different persons, who carried them off to various places South.

"Several persons in Philadelphia took an interest in Neal's case, at the time, and the sum of $3,000. was raised by them, the wife and children were purchased with the funds, and the family were re-united, and have been living in the city ever since. For the past three years, Neal had been employed as coachman by Townsend Sharpless, and it is stated, has not, during the period, been absent from his employment a single day.

"The case was brought before the Supreme Court yesterday, (Thursday, January 27th, 1853) and after some discussion it was postponed until certain papers relating thereto are received from Governor Bigler. It was rumored in the city last evening that the Governor had recalled the requisition. "

From:

"THE REPUBLICAN" [1d]

"Chester, Friday, January 28, 1853"

"To Correspondents. - - We are obliged to a friend at Media, for the particulars of a recent trial before a Justice of the Peace at that place. We are collecting some facts relative to the case, and will give them at the proper time.

'Radnor' will receive attention next week."

"The Philadelphia <u>Sun</u> contains an account of the transaction which took place in this Borough, on Monday (Tuesday, January 25th ... ed.) night last, written by Mr. Briest, a police officer, and a reporter for the press, which says: ' A crowd of all colors assembled at Goff's hotel and made sundry demonstrations.' Even the fears of a person conscious of doing wrong, could not magnify the few idlers, drawn together by the presence of a manacled man, into a ' crowd', or construe the peaceful actions prompted by their curiosity to know with what crime he was charged, into ' demonstrations to rescue'. No movement of the kind was attempted. The statement is simply a falsehood. The account then adds: 'The editor of an abolitionist paper, Mr. Walter, examined the requisition, and having explained the subject, the crowd became quiet and partly dispersed '. We did examine the requisition which had been complied with by Gov. Bigler, as well as the proceedings before Alderman Kenney - - a gentleman whom we know, and who, we presumed, would do nothing but justice in the *matter - - and we pronounced them correct; but we did not then know that the hearing had been ex parte (in the interest of one party only), and that the captors of the colored man were being hurrying him off without a fair trial. We did what we considered our duty in the case, and we are ready, at all times, to render our assistance to thwart the efforts of the man-stealers, in whatever guise they may present themselves."*

Richard's first affidavit continues:

"...... While at Chester a man came into the room, named Billy Green, with ink and paper and wanted me to tell him what I knew. I asked him what. He said I was a dammed son of a bitch. He said I insulted a gentleman last night who was my friend, and if I ever crossed his path he would knock my dammed brains out. With that he struck me with his fist on the head. I then said, you have no right to strike me. The Captain was there and said 'better let him alone he is not going to say anything'. ...."

Chapter 11

THE TRIAL

~

At the opening of the hearing, District Attorney William B. Reed telegraphed Governor Bigler's office for copies of all available documents relating to the issuing of the warrant for Richard Neal's arrest:

"*MAGNETIC TELEGRAPH OFFICE* [11]

Phila. Jan. 26.

"*Gov. Bigler,*

Please send me a certified copy of the requisition and affidavit for the surrender of Richard Neal demanded by Governor of Maryland. It is needed in a hearing before Judge Lowrie tomorrow at 10– Please send it by first mail & oblige.

W. B. Reed

Related printed news media articles:

At this point I insert multiple news articles, word for word, regarding the Supreme Court hearings, which were issued during the proceedings in

Philadelphia, by various newspapers, so that you may make your own interpretations and judgments in this case.

From the *"Pennsilvanian Inquirer"* [1d]

"COURTS"

"Thursday, Jan. 27"

"SUPREME COURT – Chief Justice Black, and Judges Lewis, Lowrie and Woodward. 'Habeas Corpus'. This morning, at about 11 o'clock, the case of Richard Neal a colored man, charged with enticing his wife and children from the service of their master, Capt. Mayo, residing in Anne Arundel county, Md., came up for hearing. The circumstances attending the arrest of Neal, and his subsequent release from the hands of the officers who had him in custody at Chester, by writ of habeas corpus, issued by Judge Lowrie, of the Supreme Court, were given in yesterdays Bulletin. He was arrested, primarily, upon a warrant directed to be issued by Gov. Bigler, upon a requisition from Gov. Lowe, of Maryland, and was on his way to that State to answer the charge of enticing slaves from the plantation of Capt. Mayo. The wife and children of Neal were manumitted several years ago, by Capt. Mayo,* for a consideration, and the alleged 'enticing away' antedates the manumission.

"F. Wharton said he wishes to call the attention of the Court to the fact of a person from Maryland having, or pretending to have, a requisition for a man now in

this city. The district Attorney has in his possession, or expects to have papers which he supposes will be part of the answer to the habeas corpus granted by Judge Lowrie.

"District Attorney Wm. B. Reed replied, that some of the friends of the defendant had made application to him last evening in reference to the mater, and he had telegraphed to Harrisburg in relation to it.

"He had received for answer, that he would receive from Harrisburg the papers relating thereto by the morning train of cars. As yet he had not received them, but held in his hand, the requisition of Gov. Bigler and a warrant of arrest issued under it by Ald. Kenney. He desired to say, that he represented the public, and not the agent from Maryland, as he had never seen or communicated with him. The papers he held had been put into his hands by Mr. Hirst, this morning, for the first time. If called upon, as a public officer, to give attention to the public business, he would do so cheerfully; but he was not prepared to make a return to the writ, as he had not seen it.

"Wm. L. Hirst said, that as his name had been mentioned in the matter, he would remark, that he had been called upon by Capt. Mayo in relation to the subject, and he had informed him, that it was a public matter, and that he had nothing to do with it. He considered it the public duty of the District Attorney to take charge of the case, as it was a requisition of one Governor to another. With this view of the subject, he handed the papers which had been put into his possession to the District Attorney.

"Judge Lowrie remarked, that the rule gave them three days to make the return.

"Judge Black said, it could not be heard until the return was made, but it would be heard as soon as that should be done, if the parties desired it.

"Mr. Hirst said, that he desired to say one other word, and that was, that the officer of the Court, with other persons, served the process of the Court upon the officers who had the prisoner in charge, demanded the custody of the prisoner under a threat of presenting the officers for a contempt of Court, if they refused to give up possession. They took him into possession, and now have him in their custody.

"Peter M'Call remarked that Mr. Lamb, the agent, immediately gave up the custody when the writ of habeas corpus was presented, and he supposed him to be the proper person to make the return.

"Judge Lewis said, that the possession should be with the person who had the original custody of the prisoner.

"Judge Black remembered, that the case was in the worst possible condition for a hearing at present. There seems to have been mutual mistakes made.

"Dist. Att'y. Reed replied, that in justice to the prisoner he would say, that the papers expected from Harrisburg would contain the affidavit sent to Gov. Bigler, upon which the requisition was issued. It was but just to the Governor too, that it should be exhibited and read.

"Mr. Wharton remarked, that if the hearing was delayed until the papers should be received from

Harrisburg, perhaps the Governor would relieve the matter of all difficulty. He thought it better to wait.

"Judge Lewis said, - I suppose the act charged against the prisoner, is a crime against the laws of Maryland.

"District Attorney Reed thought that if the case was postponed until tomorrow morning, it would be ready for a hearing.

"Judge Woodward remarked, that if the warrant now in the hands of the District Attorney was regular, the Court would not go behind the Executive warrant.

Judge Lowrie said, that the Court would hear it when the case was ready for hearing. As it was evidently not now ready, he wished to get rid of the matter until it was, and at the same time free the court room from the great crowd present. The air was exceedingly oppressive, and unpleasant.

"Judge Lewis remarked, that when the parties concerned were ready, the Court would be ready. Other public business would be postponed where the question was one of personal liberty. At present there was nothing before the Court, and he wondered why it was brought to the attention of the Court in its present condition.

"The case went over indefinitely.

The court room was crowded almost to suffocation, and the air soon became so impure within, that, cold as the weather is, the windows had to be thrown as wid(e) ly open as possible. And even this afforded but a partial relief. It is expected the case will be ripe for a hearing to-morrow (Friday) *morning.*

"There is a rumor in town that Governor Bigler has recalled the requisition."

* Mayo did not give the wife and children their freedom but sold them to the slave trader, Mr. Slaughter in Baltimore. They were eventually purchased with funds supplied by Dr. Morris, Mr. Sharpless, various abolition societies, and the husband & father, Richard Neal, who granted the wife and children their freedom.

From the Evening Bulletin, Friday, January 28th, 1853: [1d]

"EVENING BULLETIN"

Friday, January 28, 1853

"V.B. PALMER, THE AMERICAN NEWS-paper Agent, is agent for the Bulletin, and authorized to take advertisements and subscriptions at the same rates as are required by us. His offices are N. W. corner of Third and Chestnut streets, Philadelphia; Tribune Buildings, New York; M'collay's Building, Boston.

"The case of Richard Neal"

"The peculiar circumstances of the case of the nergo Richard Neal make it one of unusual interest, and its decision is looked for with anxiety by all, both in the North and the South. The fugitive slave law does not come into the controversy, as Neal is acknowledged to be a free man and is arrested as a fugitive from justice on a charge of enticing away slaves from Maryland. Such *an offence as this is one that no one who respects the laws can view with any kind of toleration. It is entirely a different affair from that of a slave himself endeavoring to escape; for this is the result of a natural instinct which no laws can control, and it would be against human nature to condemn a man for yielding to such an instinct. The aiding and abetting in the attempt to escape is a different affair, for which the constitution and laws make full provision.*

"In the complication that surrounds the case in question it is impossible to get at its true merits. All the chief circumstances of the case are as yet unsettled and in a great measure conjectural. We only know that a man who has been living here quietly for some time is seized and carried off on a charge, which is yet to be substantiated, of endeavoring to entice away slaves, the property of his former master (Richard Neal was never a slave of Captain Isaac Mayo's). *If the charge is well grounded and the requirements and formalities of the laws are properly met, justice requires that the man should be given up to the authorities of Maryland to be dealt with as her laws direct. The offence is a serious one, and it does not become Pennsylvania to throw anything in the way of the atonement which the laws of a sister State require in such a case.*

"But there are peculiar circumstances in this instance which render its decision a matter of anxious solicitude. On his arrest it was stated that Neal's offence was committed recently, while we have the word of Townsend Sharpless and other most respectable citizens, that he has not been out of the city for three

years. During this time he has been enable to purchase the freedom of his family and assemble them around him, and has led a quiet, industrious, and honest life. If such is the case, and if the former owner of his family, after suffering him to establish a home here, with his wife and children about him, and to remain for three years unmolested and unsuspecting, now comes to break up the household for an offence committed long ago, and which if ever committed, of which there is great doubt, ought and might have been tried and punished immediately after its commission - - - then we say that we can have no sympathy for the complainant, and shall not be surprised if the Pennsylvania authorities refuse to give him up. But all speculation on the subject is yet merely conjectural, and we must wait till the fog, which lawyers, governors and judges have thrown around it, is cleared away, before we can decide on the merits of the case. As it stands, it is one of painful interest, even those most anxious that Com. Mayo's rights should be respected having their sympathies excited in behalf of the man who is thus suddenly hurried from his peaceful home on a charge which is, thus far, of a most vague and unsubstantial character. "

From the *"Eve. Bulletin, Jan. 28"* [1d]

"COURTS"

Friday, Jan. 28.

"Supreme Court. - - Chief Justice Black, and Judges Lewis, Lowrie and Woodward. - - The Alleged Fugitive

From Justice - - This morning, the case of Richard Neal, an alleged fugitive from justice from the State of Maryland, was called up for hearing on the writ of habeas corpus, issued by Judge Lowrie.

"District Attorney Wm. B. Reed said he held in his hand the writ and the return of the officers who have him in custody. The writ is directed 'to Com. Mayo, and the person or persons in whose custody the prisoner is detained'. The return is as follows: -

"'To the Honorable the Judges in the annexed writ named, James Covert and John Montgomery in obedience thereto do certify and return that they have the body of Richard Neal therein named, before the said Judges as therein commanded.

"'They further certify and return that on the 26th, inst., (Wednesday) being charged with the execution of said writ they proceeded to Chester, in Delaware county whither they were informed the said Richard Neal had been removed. That on arriving at Chester they found the said Neal in custody of a person who was represented to be an officer of the State of Maryland, but whose name they do not know (John Lamb), *and Commodore Isaac Mayo, of the U.S. Navy, the prisoner Neal was handcuffed, and said the officer and the said Mayo were about removing him to the cars then about to start to Baltimore - - - that the respondent Covert produced and read the annexed writ to the officer and to Commodore Mayo - - - that the Mayo held up a paper in his hand which he said was a requisition or warrant from the Governor, that the paper was not read or its content further made known than as above mentioned. Respondents then repeated*

that they had a writ of Habeas Corpus for the said Neal, to which the officer and Captain Mayo replied that we might take the prisoner and voluntarily delivered him to us. The officer handed to us the key to the handcuffs, which were removed, and the prisoner brought in a carriage to the city of Philadelphia, where he has been in custody ever since, and is now produced to abide the order of this Court. Respondents were accompanied to the city by Commodore Mayo. They further state that they are Officers of the City Police. All which is respectfully submitted.

> *John Covert*
> *John Montgomery.'*

"'The within named James Covert and John Montgomery on their respective oaths, say that the facts in the return are true.

"'Sworn and subscribed this 28th, January,1853 before me.

> *Robt. Tyler, Prothonotary.'*

"Judge Black said, that according to the return, there did not appear to be any cause to detain the men who had the prisoner in custody. They are not the persons to whom the writ was directed.

"Dist. Attorney Wm. B. Reed - - The officers who held the writ of habeas corpus took him out of the custody of those claiming to have the requisition.

"Judge Black - - they seen to have viewed it as a writ of 'de hominem replegiando' .

"Judge Lewis - - From all that appears before us, the prisoner ought to be discharged.

"Judge Black - - Does any one appear here on the part of the person who claims to hold the prisoner. Do you, Mr. Hirst?

"Wm. L. Hirst - - Yes, Sir; I was applied to by Captain Mayo, but did not see the writ, nor have I yet seen it. Capt. Mayo has gone to Washington. He is under sailing orders in the African squadron.

"Several voices uttered the word AFRICA, emphatically, which created considerable laughter.

"Mr. Hirst - - I mean what I have said.

"Judge Black - - Do you object to the prisoner's discharge, or do you wish time to show cause for further detaining him?

"Mr. Hirst - - I appear for no one at all. The matter is in the hands of the District Attorney, to whom it properly belongs.

"Judge Black - - We have a return before us, which does not appear to hold him for any legal cause. The paper for detaining him is alleged to be in the hands of Capt. Mayo.

"Dist. Att. Reed - - Capt. Mayo called on me last evening, and I directed him to be here this morning.

"Judge Black - - Where is the person who claims to hold him as an officer of Maryland?

"Dist. Att. Reed - - I have never seen him.

"Judge Lowrie - - There has been plenty of time for any one to come forward and make claim, if there was an intention to do so.

"Dist. Att. Reed - - The return is simply the return of those persons who now hold him in custody.

"Wm. L. Hirst - - I desire to say that Capt. Mayo was not aware that he was a party named in the writ, nor did I know it until I heard it read here. I therefore ask time to telegraph him in Washington, to appraise him of the fact, and enable him to make a return to the writ.

"Dist. Att. Reed - - The writ was read to him by me.

"Mr. Hirst - - The question appears to be, whether the Court will take his return of the officers who have acted so irregularly in assuming the arrest and custody of the prisoner, or not. Capt. Mayo should have time to know how the matter stands.

"Judge Black - - Has the three days allowed by the rule of Court expired? If they have, those who hold the prisoner had better see to it.

"Judge Lewis - - They may find that they have taken a fearful responsibility upon themselves.

"P.P. Morris (Phineas Pemberton Morris, lawyer and a cousin of Dr. Caspar Morris) *- - The prisoner does not appear to be legally held in custody, and should therefore be discharged. No one claims a right to hold him here.*

"Dist. Att. Reed - - The men who executed the writ of habeas corpus, bring him here this morning to have him disposed of. Lamb, the alleged Maryland agent has never been seen in Court, nor by me, nor does he appear here to-day. When Capt. Mayo called on me last evening, I advised him of his rights, and referred him to his private counsel. I feel it to be my duty to say, that there was a

modification of the requisition, by telegraph, sent to me yesterday afternoon.

"Attorney General Campbell said, that he thought it due to the case, and to the comity that should exist between the States, that time should be allowed to the agent of the Executive of Maryland, to make a return to the writ. He was not aware that there was a present design on the part of the Executive of this State to modify or revoke, in any manner, the requisition, but questions might arise in the case requiring serious consideration.

"Mayor Gilpin - - The prisoner has been in the custody of two of my officers since yesterday, and has been kept in the City Lock-up. I did not know that my officers had served the habeas corpus until yesterday, and have been acting in the capacity of care-taker since that time for all parties. He would now say, that if the prisoner was not legally held, he would have nothing further to do with the matter, and so far as he was concerned, the prisoner was free to go about his own business.

"Judge Lowrie - - I regard it as a grave question of international policy, and as such, it should be viewed. By our rule, the persons claiming to hold the prisoner under a requisition, have three days to make a return, and the time has not yet expired.

"Att. Gen. Campbell - - I am surprised at what the Mayor of the city has just said. I hope he will reconsider his determination, and the Court will make an order that the custody of the prisoner be given to the Mayor until the return is made.

"Mayor Gilpin said, - - That if such an order was made by the Court, he would hold him.

"*Judge Lowrie, - - The prisoner ought to be held by our order until the return shall have been made, or the legal time allowed for it has expired.*

"*Judge Lewis. - - The persons who served the habeas corpus had no right to hold the prisoner; but having got him into their custody by an abuse of the writ of this Court, we ought to make an order for his safe keeping.*

"*Att. Gen. Campbell, - - I now ask the Court to make such an order.*

Mr. Hirst, - - If Capt. Mayo had supposed for a moment that the proceedings were not in accordance with the laws of Pennsylvania, he would have asked that the requisition be withdrawn, (* see copies of Governor Lowe's telegrams to William Hirst re. Mayo not withdrawling the requisition dated January 31st 1853 to follow).

"*Judge Lewis, - - He may, perhaps, be properly represented here, by stating, through counsel, whether he claims the prisoner as a fugitive or not.*

"*P.P. Morris, - - There does not appear to be any disposition to hold him, as he was given up voluntarily by Capt. Mayo to the officers who held the writ of habeas corpus.*

"*Mr. Hirst, - - Capt. Mayo will leave the whole matter with the District Attorney where it properly belongs.*

"*Dist. Att. Reed, - - The matter has been taken out of my hands by the Attorney General, and I am glad of it.*

"*Att. Gen. Campbell, - - I would not have interfered but for the statement of Mr. Reed, that he had received, by telegraph, yesterday, a modification of the requisition.*

To set the Governor right, before the Court I desire time to communicate with him.

"Judge Black, - - It appears that a Mr. Lamb was the agent of Maryland, and that he had a warrant for the arrest of the prisoner. He was therefore legally here to execute it. He was the proper one to hold him, after the arrest, or some one authorized by him. The persons who took the prisoner out of his hands acted illegally. When persons come into Court, they should ask only what the laws allow. There is no authority shown to hold the prisoner, and for his part, he had no disposition to patch up their broken vessels.

"Mayor Gilpin, - - I told Capt. Mayo that I would not be responsible for the prisoner's safe keeping.

"Judge Black, - - From what I have heard on all sides, I am satisfied that no 'mala fides' (bad faith; attempt to deceive) *was entertained by any of the parties.*

"Judge Lowrie, - - Thought there was no mistake in the matter at all, inasmuch as the agent had surrendered the prisoner willingly to be brought to Philadelphia. It was a great international question, and should be properly considered.

"P. McCall, - - The officer who had the writ of requisition, surrendered the prisoner without resistance to those who held the habeas corpus. Had it been otherwise, there might have been difficulty. The latter officers now come forward and make return. If these are the facts, he would ask the prisoner's discharge and would oppose any farther delay on the part of the Commonwealth. The case had been abandoned by the persons who originally

held him, and the return shows no cause of detainer. The prisoner is entitled to his discharge.

"Wm. L. Hirst, - - trusted it would not be on the grounds assigned by Mr. McCall.

"Judge Lewis then said, that a majority of the Court had made the following order in relation to the matter; - - ' Jan. 28, 1853, - - It is ordered, that the hearing in this case be continued until Monday morning next, at 10 o'clock, and that in the meantime, the Mayor of the City, in whose custody he (the prisoner) now is, be directed to retain him'.

"The Court room was again crowded to excess."

Two telegraphs, both dated Saturday, January 30th, 1853, at Annapolis, from Maryland's Governor, E. Louis Lowe, were sent to Captain Mayo's lawyer William L. Hirst, Esq. in Philadelphia. The first telegraph showed the Governor's willingness to consider the withdrawal of his requisition, and the second telegraph showed Capitan Mayo's refusal to back down.

First Telegraph: [11]

"The Magnetic Telegraph Company

Dated - Baltimore Jany 31 1853

Rec.d - Philadelphia, Jany 31 1853 ___-o'clock, __-min. -M

To - Wm L. Hirst Esq. Councellor at Law

"If you and Commodore Mayo will certify to me in writing that you have reason to believe that Neal is innocent of the charge, you may withdraw my requisition. Otherwise not. The crime is properly charged in the affidavit - papers are in accordance with the law. The case is within the constitution & is of a Most Serious Character, and finally the Governor of Pennsylvania has issued his warrant for the delivery of the accused. I can conceive of no circumstances to justify the with drawl of the requisition, other than your belief of Neal's innocence. Officer Lamb returned here without my knowledge or approbation. I instructed him to return to you this Saturday evening. This dispatch will be sent to Baltimore by the first mail as there is no office here.
E. Louis Lowe
Annapolis Jany 30th"

Second Telegraph: [11]

"The Magnetic Telegraph Company

Dated - Baltimore, Jan 31, 1853

Rec'd - Philadelphia, Jan 31, 1853 12 o'clock 1 min. AM

To - Wm L. Hirst Esq.

"Since my last dispatch I have seen Commodore Mayo who cannot give the required certificate. The requisition therefore cannot be withdrawn. I thought from your dispatch that Commodore Mayo was in Philadelphia.
E. Louis Lowe

Annapolis Jan 30th"

From the *"Eve. Bulletin* (Saturday) *29th of Jan."*: [1d]

"Neal, the Alleged Fugitive"

"Nothing new has come to light with regard to Richard Neal, the free colored man, seized as a fugitive from Maryland justice, and the community are waiting, in anxious suspense, the termination of the remarkable case. The doubt of the justice of Com. Mayo's charge are becoming daily more serious, and public sentiment seems to be growing in sympathy for the man torn from his family in such a sudden and violent manner. Our views on all subjects relating to the South in reference to the slave question, are all too well known to require here any new exposition of them. But while insisting, as we always have done and always shall do, that the legal rights of slave owners must be regarded in this State, we cannot lose sight of the rights of freemen.

"Now the case of Richard Neal, in its present aspect, is one that looks like an invasion of the rights of a freeman without any ground of justice or law. The offence with which he is charged must have been committed at least three years ago, if we are to believe the testimony of many respectable witnesses, who say that he has not been out of Philadelphia during all that time. He was known to be living here with his family, and yet no attempt was made to disturb him until this late period, when he is hurried away from his peaceful home, on a vague charge, and with such legal authority, as to say the least, is not free from defects. He is then driven off towards another State, where every feeling

of popular prejudice would be against him, and is only rescued by an accident from such an issue as might be expected there. But the most peculiar feature of the case is that the whole is based on the affidavit of a negro in Maryland (Mayo's slave William Hunter). *Now such testimony has no weight at all in Maryland against a white man, yet a man here, occupying the position of a white man, is seized on a serious charge, on the testimony of one who would not be a competent witness against a white man in the State where he is to be tried. These are some of the features of the matter presented in its present stage. Commodore Mayo's charge may be a correct one, but he has furnished no evidence that it is so, and all circumstances of the case are against it. If the charge is a groundless one, the wrong done to the negro will be viewed as an outrage by all who respect justice and the laws, and a feeling against slave-owners will be excited which has not heretofore existed in this law and order loving community. The case is nothing better, in its present aspect, than one of kidnapping under a legal process, and if no sufficient proof is furnished by the parties against the negro, it will be so viewed by every one. It will do much to excite the North against the South, and to destroy the good feeling and respect for the laws, which it has been our object and that of all good citizens to bring about. We look anxiously for the truth of the question to be elicited before the courts."*

From the *"North American & U.S. Gazette* (Saturday) *Jan. 29":* [1d]

"CITY ITEMS"

"NEAL, *The Alleged Fugitive From Justice. - - The case of Richard Neal, colored, the alleged fugitive from justice from the State of Maryland, was before the Supreme Court again this morning. The officers who served the habeas corpus, made return of the writ. Lamb, the agent named in the requisition, did not appear; neither did the complainant, Commodore Mayo. The case, by order of the Court, went over until Monday next so as to afford full time, and every reasonable and just accommodation to all parties concerned. The Mayor of the city was directed to retain the custody of the prisoner in the mean time.*

"We understand that Lamb, the officer who arrested the prisoner, becoming unnecessarily alarmed, in consequence of entertaining the mistaken idea that he was in danger of being roughly handled by Pennsylvania law, made a hasty flight from the city early on Thursday morning, promising to remain at Wilmington till he heard the result of the case. A Philadelphia and Chester officer went in pursuit of him, and found him at New Castle. They endeavored, in vain, to induce him to return.*

"He was unwilling to take legal advice this side of Baltimore. The Philadelphia officer, at his request, accompanied him to the Monumental city (Baltimore). Here he shamefully deceived the officer, gave him the* *slip, and left him without cent in his pocket. Some of the Baltimore Police kindly provided for their brother police-man from the North, and sent him home. Mr. Lamb's lack of moral courage was only equaled by his stupid-ity in stopping at Chester with a prisoner in irons in a closed carriage, when a drive of four or five miles further, would have placed him within the State of Delaware, beyond the reach of any Pennsylvania process. As a Maryland official, he is certainly a wonderful specimen. We are told that Commodore Mayo, highly indignant at his conduct went to look after him, yesterday."*

From the West Chester, PA, "Village Record", the following article on Tuesday, February 1, 1853: [12]

"Fugitive from Justice - Considerable Excitement"

"A colored man, named Richard Neal, was arrested on Tuesday (January 25th 1853) at the corner of Sixth and Cherry streets, by officers Lamb of Maryland, and Tapper of Spring Garden. The man was taken into custody on a requisition issued by his Excellency Governor Bigler, on a charge of being a fugitive from justice. He as taken to the Adelphi street Station house, and subsequently had a hearing before Alderman Kenny, who remanded him to the custody of Mr. Lamb, to be taken to Baltimore. Application had been previously made to the Judges of the Court of Quarter Sessions by officers, in order to

ascertain if every thing was right but Judges Allison and Thompson were absent and Judge Kelley having his hands full of civil business, had no time to attend to it. Hence the taking of the prisoner to Alderman Kenny's office. A cab was procured and the prisoner in the custody of officers Lamb, Tapper and Briest, jumped in, and off the party drove to the railroad depot, at the corner of Broad and Prime streets, Moyamensing. The cars had started about a minute and a half before the arrival of the party. It was them concluded upon to proceed to Wilmington. The roads were heavy and rugged, the air piercingly cold, and the snow falling rapidly, rendered the time gloomy in every aspect.

"The cab finally reached a place about two miles above Darby, when the prisoner suddenly sprang out and bounded off with all the agility of a deer, springing over fences, half frozen ditches, and snow covered fields. The officers with the cab driver gave chase, and such a scene of ground and lofty tumbling as took place and which has been described to us, was never seen before. It beggars description. Officer Tapper, who had practice in chasing "greasers" in Mexico, soon distanced his companions and after a chase of two miles and a half succeeded in recapturing his man. He was taken back, and shortly after dark the party arrived at Chester. Here the alarm was sounded by a colored servant at Goff's Hotel, where the party stopped to sup, that a fugitive *slave was arrested, and a crowd of all colors assembled and made sundry demonstrations to rescue.*

"With the aid of Isaiah Mirkle, a most excellent officer of Chester, the prisoner was taken from the hotel, and in the presence of the whole crowd, walked to the railroad depot, not the slightest attempt at rescue being made. The requisition having been explained the crowd became quiet and partly dispersed. On arrival of the cars at night, several persons, alleged to be officers from Philadelphia, said they had a writ of habeas corpus for Neal, but it being issued by Judge Thomson of the county of Philadelphia, the officers contended that the prisoner was outside its jurisdiction, and therefore refused to give him up. A scene now took place, in which Neal came very near being pulled to pieces.

"The cars were about to start, and knives, pistols, etc., were displayed - - sundry threats were made - - one party trying to pull Neal into the cars, and the other party trying to pull him back, in the midst of which the steam whistle of the locomotive sounded, and off went the train, leaving the prisoner and the rest of the crowd behind. Captain Mayo, of the U.S. Navy, was in the car, and on whose charge Neal was arrested. When he saw the difficulty he got out and remained at Chester.

"Yesterday morning, (Wednesday, January 26th) on arrival of the train at Chester from Philadelphia, an officer of the Supreme Court, appeared and displayed a Habeas

Corpus, issued by Justice Lowrie, of that Court. The writ of course, was promptly obeyed by the officers, and the whole party returned to Phila., the prisoner being in the custody of the officer of the Supreme Court - - He will have a hearing today (Thursday, January 27th) *at 12 o'clock.*

"The circumstances connected with this case, are alleged to be as follows: Neal was formerly a slave in the family of the Chestons, in Anne Arundel county, Maryland. He was manumitted, and after this married a female slave belonging to Captain Mayo, and subsequently removed to Philadelphia, and finally, after a deal of trouble, purchased the liberty of his wife and children, for a considerable sum of money, raised by citizens of this city. It is alleged that since that time he has enticed no less than fifteen slaves from Captain Mayo's plantation, and for this he was arrested, and not as a fugitive slave, as was first supposed. The case is now before the Supreme Court. Phila. Sun, 27th inst."

Another point of view appeared in *"THE LIBERATOR"* in Boston Mass., February 4, 1853: [13]

"ANOTHER ATROCIOUS CASE"

"P.(Philadelphia), Jan. 26. Richard Neal, a colored man, was yesterday arrested at the stables of his

employer, Mr. Townsend Sharpless, charged, on the oath
of Commodore Mayo and others, with enticing a number
of slaves from Anne Arundel county, Maryland, at
various times. According to general report, the accused
was formerly a slave in that county; his wife was a
favorite slave of the Commodore, who, on Neal obtain-
ing his freedom, gave him a farm close by, that he might
have no excuse for enticing away his wife and children.
Neal, however, moved North, and subsequently enticed
his wife and family away. They were pursued, overtaken,
and sold to go to Tennessee. It is understood, however
that his family were freed by purchase from collections
made in this city, (Philadelphia) and were living with
him here. The charge is, that Neal has visited his old
neighborhood several times since, and enticed slaves
away. The necessary requisition and other documents
were obtained, and the prisoner taken to Court; but no
judge being there, a hearing was had before Alderman
Kenney, who found the documents correct, and
remanded the prisoner into the custody of officer Lamb
of Maryland. The prisoner was taken in a vehicle to the
Baltimore depot, but the afternoon train had started,
and the officers went on to Chester, where they designed
embarking on the night mail train. Meanwhile, a writ of
habeas corpus had been obtained from judge Thompson,
and the friends of the prisoner, accompanied by members
of the Abolition Society, pursued the party to Chester.
The officers in charge of the prisoner attempted to force
him into the cars, but the friends of the prisoner and a
crowd of blacks interfered. The writ of habeas corpus in
charge of police officers from this city was presented to

officer Lamb, but in the confusion was unheeded. The parties being notified by the conductor that the train was about to start, officer Lamb, to prevent loss of life in the struggle, gave up the attempt, and lodged Neal in the lockup for the night. Another account states that the prisoner escaped, but was overtaken after being pursued 2 miles. A fresh party of officers left the city this morning (Wednesday, January 26th) *for Chester with a writ of habeas corpus from the Supreme Court. The result is not yet known.*

"Referring to the arrest of Neal, the Philadelphia 'Daily Register' makes the following comments: – We have heretofore abstained from expressing an opinion in the case of Mayo vs. Neal, hoping the warrant of extradition so hastily granted by Governor Bigler would be revoked, and that a persecution so likely to disgrace the States of Maryland and Pennsylvania would be abandoned and suffered to be forgotten. But the facts have already been spread before the world by the press. In a few days more, all Europe will have read them, and sequels to 'Uncle Tom's Cabin' will have recorded them against our civilization. In justice to our country, let them record also that no case has ever so shocked public opinion. It caps the climax of all those which have grown out of the peculiar institution. The 'Evening Bulletin', while reiterating its adhesion to the Fugitive Slave Law, pronounces this case an attempt to kidnap under legal process; and other papers are no less plain in their reprobation of Mayo's conduct. What has done more than anything else to turn the current of public opinion against Mayo is the card published in

*the 'Bulletin', by himself or his agent, as a raid adver-
tisement. In this, he parades his vindictive persecution
of Neal in a most offensive manner, and grossly insults
one of our most respected citizens, by placing his verac-
ity below that of one of the negro spies on his plantation.
The principal facts of the case may be gleamed from this
coarse and insolent statement. They are as follows: –
Richard Neal was formerly a slave in Maryland. 'Some
fifteen or sixteen years ago,' he married Matilda, who
was then Mayo's property. Acquiring his own freedom,
and unwilling to abandon his family, he rented a farm
from Mayo, and conducted it for several years, with
such industry and success as to accumulate a valuable
stock, and clear several thousand dollars. But he was
not contented. 'All of a sudden,' says Mayo, 'Neal
informed the proprietor that he must give up the farm,
as it confined him too much.' The proprietor said, 'Dick,
you intend to play me some dirty trick,' when he fell on
his knees and declared he had 'no such intention.' The
'dirty trick' alluded to was Neal's rescuing his wife and
children from slavery. Mayo had already been informed
of this design by his 'confidential servants,' or negro
spies. His fears were not at all allayed by Neal's protes-
tation; and he kept a close watch on his movements.
Some months afterwards, we find Mayo making a visit
to a farm he owned some forty miles off ('Blandair') and
taking with him, by way of precaution, Neal's wife and
her six children – rather a numerous suite for a Maryland
farmer. In a few days, Mayo returned home, leaving
Matilda and five of her children. The eldest son, 'Billy,'
accompanied him to drive his buggy. Next morning,*

*when the manager was about to give Billy a taste of
the cowhide, 'for not cleaning and feeding his horse',
Billy was not to be found. He had disappeared, and his
mother, brothers and sisters with him. The capture of
the family cost Mayo 'over $700.' The loss seems to have
waked up Mayo's spirit of revenge. His first act was to
sell the mother and her children; the next, to set on foot
means for the punishment of Neal, whom he suspected
of being accessory to the flight. Neal followed up his
wife and children, spent all he had in purchasing their
freedom, and brought them to this city, where he has
been living for three years past, respected by those who
know him as an honest, hard-working man. These facts
having come to the knowledge of Mayo, on his return
from a distant voyage, he has made one of his 'confidential servants' — whether flogged into it by the manager
or not, we do not know — testify to having seen Neal
aiding in the escape of his family. On this doubtful testimony, a requisition has been issued by the Governor of
Maryland, and complied with thoughtlessly, we regret
to say, by the Governor of this State. On one point, there
is a direct contradiction in the statement of the different
parties. Although the crime Neal stands charged with is
an unsuccessful attempt to rescue his wife and children
from slavery, — a crime never before heard of in a
civilized country, — Mayo adds that Neal has recently
tampered with his other slaves; he offers to prove it
by his negro spies, whose word, he says, 'is as good as
that of Mr. Sharpless,' one of our worthy citizens, who
has had Neal in his employ, and who states that Neal
has never left the city long enough for a trip to Anne*

Arundel county, Maryland. Granting for the sake of argument, that the negro spies and the manager, who wanted to cowhide Billy are equally credible with Mr. Sharpless, we do not think Mayo's word as good as Neal's. The former has shown himself implacable and revengeful; while we know the latter as a man who has labored the best part of his life to redeem his wife and children from slavery, and who, in his humble sphere, enjoys the esteem of all who know him. We earnestly trust that the Governor of Maryland will withdraw his requisition, or that the sages of Pennsylvania law will be broad enough to cover the intended victim.

"The Telegraph brings us the following gratifying intelligence: − P. (Philadelphia), . Jan. 31. Neal, the colored man who was arrested last week, on a charge of having incited slaves to escape, was this morning discharged by the Supreme Court, no returns having been made on the writ of habeas corpus."

From: *"The Jeffersonian"* West Chester, PA, dated February 5, 1853: [12]

"The Case of Richard Neal"

"On Tuesday (February 1st), before Chief Justice Black, and Judges Lewis, Lowrie and Woodward, Richard Neal was brought into Court by the Mayor's officers, who held him in custody by order of the Supreme Court, A considerable crowd was in attendance.

"After the Court was opened, Judge Black said – we know what this crowd means here. Mr. Wharton, has a return been made to the writ of habeas corpus?

"Fr. Wharton – I believe not, sir. We have nothing to say, but ask for the prisoner's discharge.

"P. M'Call – There has been no return to the writ.

"Judge Lewis – He ought to be discharged then.

"Judge Black – I don't see that we have anything to do with the matter. There is nothing before us.

"Judge Lewis – The prisoner is held in custody by our order, and we should discharge him. Let him be discharged.

"P. M'Call – Richard, you may go.

"Richard, surrounded by rejoicing friends of both colors, left the room in high spirits. A portion of the crowd lingered behind, as if dissatisfied with the short turn the case had taken."

During the hearings feelings had become so aroused among the Neal supporters that, without Dr. Morris' knowledge, Peter McCall, Pemberton Morris and Francis Wharton procured a warrant for the arrest of Commodore Mayo as a perjurer and for attempted Kidnapping of a negro. When Dr. Morris was told of this in Mr. Wharton's office he stated that he would have no part in anything that would appear to be retaliation, the only thing he would do was to protect Richard Neal. After reading the warrant carefully Dr. Morris quietly took the fireplace poker and held the warrant in the fire with it until it was completely burned.

There was no further effort to charge Commodore Mayo with any misdoings.

On Tuesday, February 8th, 1853, there appeared the following article in the West Chester, PA "Village Record": [12]

"The Case of Neal. - - Richard Neal, the colored man who was recently arrested on a requisition from the Governor, charged with enticing slaves from Maryland, has been discharged, no one appearing against him on the hearing before the Supreme Court, in Philadelphia on Monday week (January 30th,1853). *The alleged offence was committed three years ago, and has been suffered to lie over till the present time, when the man was suddenly seized and hurried off, without any chance to vindicate himself. It was only through the vigilance of his friends that he was recovered before reaching Maryland; and now, since publicity had been given to the facts through the press, those who brought the charge are either ashamed or afraid to come forward and make it good. - - There is something wrong about this whole affair, and Governor Bigler should have it properly investigated. If the charge was only a ruse to get possession of the man, as in the recent case of Rachael and Elizabeth Parker, Gov. Bigler ought to issue another requisition for the parties concerned on a charge of attempting to kidnap. This is quite as heinous an offence as that alleged against Neal of enticing his wife and children from slavery. - - If the rule of law does not work both ways, it is not the rule of justice."*

A terse report from Washington D.C., *"The National Era, February 10, 1853"*: [14]

*"**DISCHARGE OF NEAL, -** Philadelphia, Jan.31. - Richard Neal, the negro man charged with enticing slaves from Anne Arundel county, Md., was this morning discharged from custody by the Supreme Court, the agent of Maryland not being in attendance."*

Chapter 12

THE AFTERMATH

Except for the kind heart of Dr. Caspar Morris, Commodore Mayo would have been tried for attempted kidnapping.

From the *"Eve. Bulletin* (Wednesday) *Feb. 2"* [1d]

"The Case of Richard Neal"

"To the Editor of the Evening Bulletin:

"Dear Sir - - The courtesy you have extended to me in withholding from your columns any matter adapted to stimulate still further the feeling of this community in reference to the case of Richard Neal, induces me to trespass still further on your kindness by soliciting a place for the following statement of facts of the case so far as I am interested in or informed of them. A similar narrative has been transmitted to the Governor of Maryland, and the main facts of the case were stated a few days since to Governor Bigler.

  Yours truly,   *Caspar Morris*

*"In the month of May, 1843, James Cheston, Esq.,
merchant of Baltimore, and Planter of West River, Anne
Arundel county, Maryland, being previously in good
health, was seized suddenly with disease of the heart, of
which he died after a few hours illness. He had always
been anxiously interested in promoting the welfare of
his slaves, but was deterred from manumitting them by
a belief that it would not be an advantage to them. His
first care when informed of the approach of death, was
for his negroes, and the first article in a nuncupative
will was, ' I commit my servants to my sons, not as
property, but that they may make such disposition of
them as shall most conduce to the benefit of said slaves',
thus transferring to his children the same trust he had
himself discharged. No other persons than his physician
and said family being present, this will proved invalid
and the property passed into the hands of the Chancery
Court, and the servants, as well as the other personal,
and the real estate, were divided by Commissioners. The
family, with perfect unanimity, determined that, under
all the circumstances of the case, the slaves of able body
and over twenty one years of age and below the age* (of
45) *limited by the law of the State of Maryland, should
be immediately manumitted, and each of the* (Cheston)
*heirs executed the necessary papers for those allot-
ted to them.*

*"At the time at which I announced to the people on
my farm the fact that they were no longer slaves, but at
liberty to seek other employ, or remain in mine, as they
wished. I directed their attention to the fact that the eyes
of the whole neighborhood would be fixed upon their*

behavior, and that any attempt on their part to inter-fere with the relations of the masters and their slaves, would only involve themselves in danger, and ourselves in difficulty; and that while I would ever be their friend in case they conducted themselves with propriety, they need never expect me to do anything for them if they involved themselves in difficulty by any such interfer-ence; and at each of my subsequent visits to the estate I have reiterated the same advice and assurance.

"Among those who fell to the share of my wife (Anne Cheston Morris) *was Richard Neal, then about thirty years old, in perfect health and remarkable for his docil-ity and faithfulness - - traits which also marked in an eminent degree his mother, still living on my farm in a highly confidential position, and his father a confiden-tial slave of the late Hon. Virgil Maxey. Richard had, while himself a slave, married a woman named Matilda, the slave of Commodore Isaac Mayo, who possessed an estate lying contiguous to that of Mr. Cheston, and now in my possession, from which it is separated by an inlet from the Bay of more than one mile wide.*

"Soon after his manumission Richard, confident of being able to occupy his time and strength to better advantage for himself than in my service, left my employ and rented from Commodore Mayo an island, of the precise extent of which I am ignorant, for the sum of one hundred and twenty five dollars per annum, which he cultivated during about three years, more or less. At the end of that time, not finding it so profitable as he had hoped, he abandoned it, receiving at the time of his final settlement with Commodore Mayo, the sum

of about three dollars. What other profit he had derived from the cultivation I cannot know, but am confident that the estimate of ' several thousand of dollars', made in a statement published in the Bulletin by some one representing the cause of Commodore Mayo, must be an excessive exaggeration, unless the poor negro, with little capital accumulated by catching and selling oysters during his leisure hours and at night, while in slavery, was a much more accomplished and successful planter than his late master is.

"Soon after the abandonment of the island, a feeling of suspicion of Richard and irritation toward Matilda, was manifested by Commodore Mayo, which gave rise to frequent complaints on the part of Matilda, of the treatment to which she was subjected, until at length, two of her fellow slaves having been sold, and she herself threatened with the same fate, she in an evil hour, in the autumn of 1849, attempted to abscond with her children. She and her younger children were at the time at an estate of Commodore Mayo's (Blandair at Elk Ridge, MD), *near Baltimore. That Richard was not with them has always asserted and can, I believe, prove. My first information of the running away and subsequent arrest was derived from Richard, who presented himself at my house in Philadelphia, and announced these facts, I at once recalled to his recollection the advice I had given him and his fellow servants, and told him I could not assist him out of the trouble he had brought upon himself. In reply he assured me in the most solemn manner, that he was not only not an abettor of the act, but that he had always discouraged her when she would talk of it, under the influence of her*

grievances; and that he knew nothing of it till he heard of her arrest, on which he had come directly to me for relief. He informed me, in addition, that he had more than five hundred dollars, which he had saved himself, which he would give for her redemption, and sell himself and family (indenture himself and family) *to me till he could work out the balance, if I would advance the sum requisite for their purchase. - - Un willing to do this, but anxious to relieve a fellow being from the most intense anguish of which nature is susceptible, in conjunction with my family, and by the assistance of liberal friends, a sufficient sum was quickly raised to purchase the wife and youngest child, and they were bought by an agent from the trader* (Mr. Gordon) *to whom the whole family had been sold by Commodore Mayo, on recovering possession of them, (who thus received their full value) and brought at once to this city. - - The purchase was affected after they had left Baltimore, at a stopping place by the road side, the mother and child being taken from the cars as though to get breakfast for the family, and the other children carried on the route for Tennessee. The sad idea of the separation of so young and helpless a family from both parents together with their impression, communicated by Matilda, that her children were to be separated from each other when finally sold, solicited so much feeling in Philadelphia, New York and Boston, that the funds necessary were raised and forwarded to an agent* (Mr. Gullion) *who bought the children in Virginia after they had left Richmond; and they were all once more united in a new home. The cost of the whole transaction exceeded three thousand dollars. Richard was immediately taken into employ of Mr. Townsend Sharpless, first as a jobber, and then as his coachman, and has continued here to deserve the same high character he had acquired while a slave, and which had induced Commodore Mayo to rent him land. His repeated assertion that instead of encouraging his wife to attempt her escape, he had always opposed it, my confidence in his integrity, his perfect propriety of deportment, and my belief in his readiness to bide by my instructions, repeatedly given, to keep himself entirely free from any association with Abolition efforts, had given me perfect confidence in his security. I no more dreamed of danger to him than to myself. I had repeatedly urged him to emigrate to Liberia, because I think that is the proper refuge of the negro race, and for that reason only, little suspecting that the outrage which has excited so much feeling, could be perpetrated at mid-day in our city.*

"On the afternoon of the 25th. of January I was thee miles from my residence, in the upper part of the district of Kensington, at the Hospital of the Protestant Episcopal Church, where I was startled by a messenger who brought me a note from home, announcing merely Richard had been arrested by Commodore Mayo, and it was believed had been conveyed out of the city. It was then nearly six o'clock. Hastily returning to town, I first ascertained that the party had not left by the two o'clock train of cars; that there was some legal process in the case; but what was the crime charged, and what the nature of the process I could not learn. After visiting several magistrate's offices, and calling at the police station, I could obtain no information except that it was for abducting slaves; the time when this was alleged to

have been done I could not learn. I did learn, however, that the process had been most summary. That no opportunity had been afforded for information to reach either myself, his former master, or Mr. Sharpless his recent employer. That just in time to accomplish the purpose before the starting of the cars, and therefore apparently with the design of keeping us ignorant of the whole proceeding until he should be beyond the reach of our assistance he had been carried away, while circumstances of the most aggravating nature were reported to have marked the conduct of those engaged in the affair.

"But a short space of time remained. I therefore at once secured counsel, and taking out a writ of <u>habeas corpus</u> proceeded with an officer to the Prime street depot, hoping to find the party there. Disappointed in this, and compelled to return to patients extremely ill, who required my immediate attention, the writ was entrusted to an officer who accompanied by two citizens, proceeded with it in the train, thinking it possible, rather than hoping to find the party had pursued the course they did. Unarmed, except in that divine panoply in which 'he is thrice armed who has his quarrel just', they reached Chester just in time to prevent, by the interposition of this writ the further abduction of Richard.

"Upon this presentation, and not till then, was it discovered that the only ground on which the writ of requisition of the Governor of Maryland was issued was and out of which all these painfully exciting events have grown, was the oath of one slave of Commodore Mayo, made after a lapse of more than three years, that Richard Neal was present and aided in the attempt of his wife to

escape in the year 1849. No charge was brought of any crime of a subsequent date.

"Having thus in a manner they supposed to be perfectly lawful caused the detention of Richard, the citizens, officers, &c. returned in the up train, and by dint of untiring exertion procured a writ from the Supreme Court of the State, requiring the presentation of Richard to that body.

"Such is a succinct history of the whole course of events from the emancipation of Richard Neal, to the attempt, under cover of legal proceedings, to abduct him from his home. The only purpose now entertained is to place the public in possession of the main features of the case, and to exonerate the State of Pennsylvania and the citizens of this vicinity from the imputation of any purpose to thwart the course of justice or to prevent its due administration. To those whom I am know I need not state my views regarding slavery and its co-relative subjects. To them I may refer, however, those who do not know me for proof of the assertion that I am not, and never have been in any way associated with Abolitionism, Free Soilism, or any of the associated agencies which have been productive of so much mischief to the negro race, and have so fearfully agitated our whole nation. As regards the allegation made in the Card in your paper of the 27th. ult. that 'another of the Cheston freed negroes has been arrested for an attempt to entice away his wife'. I know not what connection it can have with the present case, unless it be to attempt to prejudice the public against Richard by visiting on him the sins of all who may have been born on the same

plantation. The true state of the case is, that the man had married a woman who was a slave for a term of years. That term has expired. He alleges that she is unjustly withheld from him; and has brought suit in the courts at Annapolis for her. - - - Whether a cross action has been resorted to, leading to his arrest, on such a charge, I know not. The notice of the case in the advertisement was first intimation of such proceeding reaching me."

"CASPAR MORRIS"

Editors Note: – I have not found the identity of the second Cheston free negro accused of attempting to entice his wife to run away from her owner purportedly after her term of bondage had expired.

From the *'Batlo. Sun" - un dated* (Feb. 2, 1853)

"THE RICHARD NEAL CASE - - Messrs. Editors - - Please copy the subjoined statement of the facts in this case, made by Dr. Caspar Morris, of Philadelphia, and published in the 'Evening Bulletin'. It is a most temperate statement and omits points that would strongly exhibit the true character of the late proceedings against this man. He is discharged, however, and it is perhaps not needful now to bring them before the public. I will only encroach on your columns further to say, that since the absconding, arrest, and sale of Richards wife in 1849, he has never been within the limits of the State of Maryland. Also, in notice of threats made of the 'Cheston free negroes' in a counter statement before the

public as though they were a nuisance, it is but just to them to state that they were manumitted nine years ago, consisting then of about 80 individuals. Not one of them set at liberty has ever required assistance of their former owners, been chargeable on the public, or arraigned before a court for a violation of the laws. They have maintained themselves by their honest industry.

G. C. (Galloway Cheston?)

"From The Philadelphia Bulletin

Richards Neal's Case - - We had intended to make some remarks on the case of the negro Richard Neal, but we have received a statement from Dr. Caspar Morris which so fully covers the ground that it is unnecessary for us to comment on it. We publish the statement, and do not doubt that it will be universally read. Dr. Morris stands so highly here; and his course in reference to all such questions as this has been so honorable, that the utmost confidence will be placed in all he says."

(Note: See Dr. Morris's statement under "Evening Bulletin" - preceeding pages 127 thru 135, dated Feb. 2nd.)

From the:

"EVENING BULLETIN [1d]*"*

WEDNESDAY, FEBRUARY 2

Richard Neal Discharged

"By reference to the court proceedings, it will be seen that the case of Richard Neal came on this morning

before the Supreme Court. No one appeared against him, and he was discharged, thus leaving the case in a very suspicious position."

From the *"Phila. Sun* (Friday) *Feb. 4th 1853:"* [1d]

"LOCAL MATTERS"

"The Case of Officer Tapper, - - We notice in our last, the arrest of Mr. Charles Tapper, of the Marshal's police, on complaint of Richard Neal, for assault and battery, committed when Neal attempted to escape from his custody, while conveying him to Chester, in a carriage. We stated that Alderman Mitchell, after some remarks, held Mr. Tapper to bail. In justice to the Alderman, and that the peculiar case may be understood, as it will doubtless elicit extended inquiry into police powers, we give the remarks of the Alderman. After Neal had given his evidence, Alderman Mitchell said:

'It always gives me pain to issue a warrant against any officer of the city and county of Philadelphia, as I know that they are sometimes censured if they do their duty, and also when they neglect to do it. But the defendant, according to the evidence in this case, has allowed his feelings to go beyond his duty in my opinion. And I sit here, in virtue of my office, to do justice to all parties, without respect to color, and as the same God made Richard Neal that made us all, and our laws allow him the same right, I must protect him when wrongfully assaulted. You know, that if his case had been ours, and we had been arrested without knowing for what, taken

away from our friends, without them being allowed to have notice, and hurried among those we feared might do us injury, we would have used all means in our power to escape. I am no <u>Abolitionist</u>, but a <u>stern lover of justice</u>, and I have my own views of this case as to the legal right of all the city officers concerned in it. The Marshal's Police are deputed to attend to certain duties and districts, and when absent, those districts are left un protected, and I think it a matter for investigation by proper tribunal, whether my views are right or wrong on this subject. I have no wish to be served in this case, and will only ask five hundred dollars bail.'"

From:

"THE REPUBLICAN [1d]
"CHESTER, FRIDAY, FEBRUARY 4, 1853.

"The Case of Richard Neal. - - The case of the colored man, Richard Neal, who was detained at this place last week on writ of habeas corpus, the facts relating to which we gave in our paper on Friday (Jan. 28th) was brought to a close on Monday by the discharge of the prisoner - - - his persecutors, Mayo and Lamb, failed to appear against him, having suddenly left the City for the South. This attempt to <u>kidnap</u> a free colored man is one of the boldest of the kind of which we have any knowledge, and we therefore sum up the facts of the case in order to show who are the guilty parties in it. Mayo, it seems, applied to Gov. Lowe, of Maryland, on the oath of a slave - - - an obligation which has no

*binding force in that State - - - charging Richard Neal
with attempting, some three years ago, to incite his own
wife and children, slaves of Mayo, to run away from
their master, and join him (Neal) who was then free and
residing in Philadelphia. A requisition on Governor
Bigler* (of Pennsylvania) *was made on this ground for
his surrender into the hands of the Maryland authorities, which was granted by the Executive of our State
without examination into the merits of the case, and by
his order the man is seized, handcuffed, and dragged
before a magistrate - - a partial hearing is had, and he is
consigned to the tender mercies of his captors. Secure of
their prey, they seek the cars for Baltimore, but finding
themselves a minute or two late, they proceed in their
close-covered wagon to Chester, on reaching which they
turn down a bye-street to an out-of-the-way tavern,
with the prisoner securely pinioned and closely guarded.
When asked by some of our citizens the nature of the
prisoner's offence, and by what authority he is held in
custody, they exhibit the requisition from Gov. Bigler,
bearing the broad seal of the State, and are unmolested
by the law-abiding people here. In the mean time the
rumor is abroad in Philadelphia, that RICHARD NEAL
- - - a man who had been faithful to his employer, and
by his upright conduct had gained the good opinion of
all who knew him - - - had been secretly captured and
hurried off. His friends exerted themselves in his behalf,
and armed with the proper commission, they overtake
him at this place, just as his captors are about to debark
with him for the South. They present their warrant, and
ask his detention, and for so doing are threatened with*

*the contents of his deadly weapons held by Capt. Mayo
and his aiders and abettors, in the business of kidnapping. Neal is subsequently taken back to Philadelphia,
and after undergoing imprisonment for nearly a week,
he is told by the Court that there is no charge against
him - - - he may go! On the return of Mayo and his
party to the city, they found the climate too hot for their
comfort, and they accordingly leave between two days,
and have not been heard of officially since. It is said that
Mayo has gone to join the <u>African</u> squadron, to which
he has been ordered previous to this attempt on his part
to raise the wind by abducting a free man. We take it
he is a marvelous proper officer for our Government to
send out to suppress the slave trade. He, an officer of the
United States Navy! - - - a Navy which has ever boasted
of its gallant men. He, the Navy officer who flourished his loaded pistol over the heads of peaceable and
unarmed citizens - - he it was who threatened to blow
out the brains of those who were engaged in uphold-
ing the supremacy of the law. We call upon President
Fillmore to rid the Navy of such a <u>gallant</u> officer, by
striking his name from the roll, without ceremony. He
should be taught that the man-stealer's mission does not
comport with the soul of chivalry and honor which we
are told is covered by the gilded epaulette of the Navy.
It will be asked abroad whether this is the valiant man,
who, caught in a disgraceful act, and becoming alarmed
at the law's majesty, ingloriously fled to avoid convic-
tion. We beg the President to have respect for the right
arm of our country's defense, and remove the blot which
his retention in the ranks of the Navy will cast upon it.*

"It will be seen from the proceedings in the (State) *Senate, which we publish in this paper, that a preamble and resolution was submitted last week by Mr. Kunkle, calling upon Governor Bigler for his reasons for complying with the requisition of the Governor of Maryland. What apology our Governor may give for his share in the proceedings, if indeed he consents to give any, remains to be seen. The question involved is one of importance to every resident in the State, white or colored, bond or free. The people have some interest not only in the making of laws, but in the way in which they are executed. It behooves them to look closely into every transaction effecting personal liberty, and to denounce every act of swift and arbitrary power that renders that liberty uncertain and insecure. One successful stretch of power like this, makes a precedent for a second, and a jealous and vigilant eye should at all times be directed towards the exercise of such power in the hands of the Executive. On this point there is an abundance of admonition and example in times past. We are all familiar with the operation of the 'Letters de Catchet', issue by the French monarchy, which seized a man without warning or accusation, fettered and gagged him, transported him to the Bastile, and there entombed him forever. Poison or the dagger often finished what tyranny began.*

"The debate in the Senate that there is a mawkish sensibility on the part of some Senators who took part in the proceedings on the resolution of Mr. Kunkle. These gentlemen appear to be alarmed lest the good people of Pennsylvania should be 'agitated' by any movement on

the subject, on the part of the Legislature. If a citizen or a 'resident' - - - we presume the latter is the polite word, particularly if a man's skin is a little colored - - - can be seized by an order from the Governor, based upon a requisition from another Governor, founded on the qualifications of a single unqualified witness, for an offence unknown to our laws, fettered, shut up in a carriage or railway car, and hurried off to be heard of no more, it is high time that the people should be 'agitated' - - - high time for them to inquire, and to know whether they live under a Republican government - - - whether the 'one man power' is supreme, or not. What has happened to RICHARD NEAL might happen to the whitest banker or merchant - - - to the Mayor of Philadelphia, himself. There are miscreants enough, unhappily, to applaud such proceedings, and to talk about revolvers and other deadly weapons, but it chanced, however, in this borough, that they belong to the minority, and were therefore harmless.

"We hope Mr. Kunkle will call up his resolution at an early day. If the Governor treats the Senate so disrespectfully as to refuse to answer, let his supporters in the body defend him, if they can, and explain why he backed out so suddenly."

From the Philadelphia *"Sunday Dispatch, Feb. 6th"*, 1853 [1d]

"KIDNAPPING BY LAW"

"Whilst the people of the North should persevere in the determination to uphold and support the Fugitive Slave Law, they should keep a jealous eye

upon the movements of slaveholders to compass their designs by fraudulent employment of the forms of law. Human liberty is a blessed boon, whether those who seek it are black or white, and it is the duty of every citizen to endeavor to preserve the right of freedom for himself and all others. The last ten days has witnessed the commencement and conclusion of one of the most extraordinary proceedings which the forms of law have ever been called upon to sanction. We refer to the case of Richard Neal, the circumstances of which are well known to most of our readers. Neal had the misfortune to have been born a slave, but was manumitted. His wife was the bondwoman of Commodore David (Isaac) Mayo, of the United States Navy, a man who, probably, considers himself 'an officer and a gentleman', and claims respect upon account of his station. The naval officer, it would seem from the revelations which have been made, is haughty, tyrannical, and malicious. He took some dislike against the wife of Neal. He ill-treated her, and she attempted to runaway. The husband was not with her, and disavows all knowledge of the transaction. The woman and her children, were caught, and then the 'brave Commodore' determined to sell them into a state of slavery far south. The negotiations were effected, and the transfer made, but the white friends of Neal interfered, rescued the mother and one child, and subsequently regained the other children. Neal came to this city with his family, and has since lived an honest, sober, and industrious life.

"It would have been thought that the concern of 'the officer and gentleman', with his late fugitives, would

have ceased with their sale. He had disposed of them; he had received his price, and for the sum it would have been thought he released all grievances of which he had cause to complain. The offence of his servants in endeavoring to escape was atoned for, and he had received value for the injury done his right of property. The wife of Neal could not be punished by him, and whatever his former cause of complaint, it is fair to say that his future silence was <u>purchased</u>. No honorable man, after such a settlement, would trouble himself about the business. There is no way of accounting for the subsequent conduct of 'the officer and gentleman' other than by supposition that he is <u>not</u> honorable.

"He nurses his wrath for three years. He allowed his malice to simmer for that time over the coals off his discontent, to keep it warm. He must have considered long and pondered well the means of carrying out his spite, and, finally, despairing of honest means, determined to resort to fraud. His victim was Richard Neal, the husband and father of his quondam slaves. Against that man 'the gallant Commodore' had no evidence whatever which was worth a pin by the laws of Maryland. Foiled in his desires by the want of legal testimony, the 'officer and gentleman' did not hesitate to resort to that which was illegal. One of his own slaves was induced to make oath that Neal had incited his wife to run away. Whether the complicity of the negro with the designs of his master was effected by threats, violence, or by cajolement and promises is unknown, but certain it is that, by the laws of Maryland, the oath of the slave against the freeman, Neal, was utterly worthless. The commodore

knew this well, but he seems to have been determined to effect his purpose, however base the fraud be which was necessary to compass it. With the oath of the bondman, he was able to obtain a requisition by the Governor of Maryland upon the Governor of Pennsylvania, for the body of Richard Neal, upon a charge of inciting a slave to run away - - - an offence unknown to our laws, and one which we venture to assert lies not within the comity between this State and our Southern sister. That view of the case was, of course, no obstacle in the way of the Maryland dignitary. Negro law overrides every statue in that Commonwealth, and anything which touches the interest in human chattels is of the utmost importance.

"We wish we could say that the Governor of Pennsylvania was as careful of the liberty of those residing in the State as he should have been. Probably he was dazzled by the title or the uniform of 'the officer and gentleman'. Very little inquiry could have been made whether the offence which was charged was one which is within the provisions of the Constitution. The character of the witness upon whose simple oath the whole proceeding was based, could not have been examined into by Governor Bigler. Anxious to sub-serve the wishes of the Maryland authorities - - - desirous of showing them that Pennsylvania is willing to go beyond constitutional requirements in order to please the South - - - the gallant commodore was received at Harrisburg with complaisance and smiles. The trumped up charge was not too nicely examined. The fraudulent accusation, which had no strength in law, was not tested. A

sort of blindness must have struck the Executive. The consideration which was due to the subject could not have been extended. Governor Bigler yielded at once to the charm of the sign manual of his Southern guberna-torial brother, when that charm was enhanced by the presence of 'the officer and gentleman'. A warrant for the capture of poor Dick Neal was granted and, armed with that authority, the 'brave Commodore' came to Philadelphia. The proceedings were planned with the same cunning which had distinguished the officer of the Navy throughout. Neal was arrested at an hour which gave his captors sufficient time to hurry him before an Alderman, who hurried through the formalities, when the victim was hurried to the railroad depot in order to be hurried off to Baltimore.

"As 'the best laid plans of mice and men gang aft agley,' it happened, in this case that the 'officer and gentleman' over reached himself. There was a little mistake in the calculation of the time necessary to consummate the transaction; it took too long; and when the party reached the Baltimore railroad station the cars had gone. A carriage ride to Chester was the only method left, and to this circumstance the subsequent rescue of the man is to be attributed. The friends of Neal, armed with a habeas corpus followed in the evening train, and overtook the officer of the navy, and his victim, at Chester. Here an altercation ensued, the cars went off, leaving pursuers and pursued there, and subsequently the colored man was brought to this city.

"We have said that the course of the 'officer and gentleman' evidenced malice, fraud, and cunning. The

history of the case now adds cowardice to these. 'The brave commodore' abandoned the business the moment that the rescuers overtook him. His Baltimore police officer ran away, and dared not trust his precious body in the Commonwealth of Pennsylvania. The 'officer and gentleman' had not nerve sufficient to return to Philadelphia and face the censures of an indignant community. He <u>sneaked away</u> from the consequences of his own malicious proceedings, and has gone no one knows whither. The man Neal was discharged, because no one was bold enough to sustain the illegal and fraudulent charge which Commodore Mayo had trumped up against him; and thus ended this extraordinary chapter in Philadelphia history.

"In regard to Commodore (Isaac) Mayo, of the United States Navy, no words can be strong enough to express the contempt which his conduct has excited in every liberal mind. He has stooped to acts, which not only disgraces him but the uniform which he wears. He has imposed upon the Executives of two States by a fabricated affidavit, which he knew to be perfectly worthless. He has invoked the forms of law to carry out his fraud and malice. He attempted to carry off a freeman by force and violence, only appealing to the law as a shield for his own trickery; and finally, when resistance gathered, the world saw the curious spectacle of an American officer running away from the victim whom he tried to seize, and making himself safe among kindred spirits. Will the American Navy allow itself to be disgraced by the continuance of this officer in commission? Is it not the duty of the Secretary of the Navy to order a court marshal

*to determine whether the conduct of Commodore Mayo
in this matter was becoming to 'an officer and a gentleman?' The character of the Navy depends upon the
behavior of the officers. If they are guilty of impropriety
in private life, they will not be respected by reason of their
position in the service. Could not Commodore Mayo be
arrested for kidnapping? The fraudulent invocation of
the forms of law to carry out a deceit ought to be no
protection to any one. Such a course is only an aggrava-
tion of the wrong. We trust that something will be done
on this point by the friends of Richard Neal. It is time to
teach the south that, although attention and respect will
be paid to their constitutional rights, the spirit of a free
people will always interpose itself to protect the freeman
in his liberty."*

From the *"Germantown Telegraph"* - no date. [1d]

"THE CASE OF RICHARD NEAL"

*"Richard Neal, the colored man, coachman to
Townsend Sharpless, of Philadelphia, who was recently
arrested on a requisition of the Governor of Maryland
upon the Governor of this State, has been discharged,
no one appearing against him on the hearing before the
Supreme Court, though the case was twice postponed
to accommodate the Maryland party, with Commodore
Mayo at their head. The alleged offence, consisting in
an attempt on the part of Neal to entice his wife and
children, then slaves, to run away from their owner, was
committed three years ago, and has been suffered to lie
over till the present time, when the man was suddenly*

seized and hurried off without any chance to vindicate himself. It was only through the vigilance of his friends that he was recovered before reaching Maryland; and now, since publicity has been given to the facts through the press, those who brought the charge are either ashamed or afraid to come forward and make it good. There is something wrong about this whole affair, and Governor Bigler should have it properly investigated. If the charge was only a ruse to get possession of the man, as in the recent case of Rachel and Elizabeth Parker, Gov. Bigler ought to issue another requisition for the parties concerned on a charge of attempt to kidnap. This is quite as heinous an offence as that alleged against Neal of enticing his wife and children from slavery. If the rule of law does not work both ways, it is not the rule of justice.

"We are glad to see that Mr. Kunkle has brought the subject before the Senate, which body has adopted a preamble and resolution, requesting the Governor to furnish the Senate with copies of the indictment, affidavit, requisition and correspondence upon which the order for the arrest was found. We hope the matter will be thoroughly sifted, in order that we may know the whole truth, let the censure fall where it may. To us it is very clear, that our authorities, in their anxiety to conciliate the South in relation to slavery, are ready to concede everything to it, even the invasion of our soil, and the carrying off of our citizens, without the pretence of justification.

"It is indeed time that we should look about us and guard our rights. The free States certainly have or ought

to have, <u>some</u> rights too. Let us adhere faithfully to the 'compromise' - - - to the Constitution - - - but let us guard the freedom of our soil with sleepless watchfulness, that it shall never, under any circumstances, become the highway of slavery. We think that the Representatives of the People at Harrisburg, are too strongly imbued with the spirit of humanity and justice, and are too mindful of the respect due to the character and position of Pennsylvania, not to resist, with manly independence, any attempt to degrade her, by an abandonment of this spirit, this respect, and this position, and pacing her as effectually at the service of the South, in supporting the 'institution', as though it had never been abolished within her limits. Let the case of RICHARD NEAL - - - of RACHEL and ELIZABETH PARKER, be kept before the Legislature - - - and we have no fear that the sympathy for slavery will multiply our laws in its favor."

As time passes, details in the press become clearer and more complete:

From *"Correspondence of the New York Evangelist"* [1d]

"NEAL, THE COLORED MAN"

"Philadelphia, Feb. 7th. 1853."

"Your brief notice in the Evangelist of last week, of the case of Richard Neal, a free colored man, whose abduction, under peculiarly aggravated circumstances, was attempted, but happily frustrated, requires some amplification to give your readers a just view of its malignant

atrocity. Dr. Caspar Morris has published a statement of the case, but there are other facts connected with it which should be pondered, to illustrate the tenure by which thousands of our defenseless citizens hold the dearest blessings of life.

"1. The basis of this whole proceeding rests upon the oath of a slave on Commodore Mayo's plantation in Maryland. Maryland officers received the oath of a Maryland slave which in Maryland is good for nothing; and upon this worthless evidence, which is not admitted against a citizen of the State, the Governor of Maryland issues his requisition upon the Governor of Pennsylvania for a free citizen of our free State. Gubernatorial comity, or some other occult principle, demands the sacrifice, and the victim is yielded up.

"2. The circumstances attending the arrest, develop an exquisite refinement in malignity. The arrest it self was adroitly accomplished. The hand of a master was in it. When Commodore Mayo thought his victim secure, he went at once to the house of Neal to see Matilda, the wife of Neal, and his former slave. She was not at home - - only the children were there. The gallant Commodore remorselessly opened his battery upon them, broadside after broadside. He told them he had caught their father at last - - - that he had sent him off to the South - - - that he would be sold as a slave for life - - - that they would never see him again, and, said he, '<u>tell your mother I say so and I wish she was here that I might tell her so myself.</u>' The victorious Commodore, leaving the poor frightened children, started for the main prize, in chase of a police-man. His absence relieved the terrified children, and

nerved by despair, they ran to their father's friend, Dr. Morris, and to Mr. Sharpless, in whose service he was employed. These gentlemen promptly and nobly met the emergency. The Commodore is a bad tactician. He overreached himself. His malignity, true to its nature, was blind. Had he been content to inflict the anguish without going to Neal's house and gloating over it, to the utter terror of his children, he would have preserved the character of the U.S. Navy from so deep a stigma of infamy, and yet have accomplished his nefarious purpose. But now his own wickedness betrays him, and 'his violent dealing comes down on his own pate!'.

"3. The rescue is not without interest. The 'Habeas Corpus' was obtained, but nowhere could the man be found. Time would not admit of extended search, and two gentlemen, the sons of Dr. Morris, and Mr. Sharpless, accompanied by a police officer, left with the first train of cars for Baltimore. On arrival at Chester, sixteen miles below Philadelphia, Neal was found, and the writ served. Unfortunately it was issued by an officer whose jurisdiction was limited to the county line, and it was therefore resisted. One of the pursuers grasped Neal firmly, exclaimed, 'This is my man'! Commodore Mayo in an instance drew a pistol, and threatened to blow out his brains. 'Fire if you dare,' nobly responded the young man. 'You are now in a free State, fire if you dare'. The brave Commodore thought it prudent to decline the challenge he had provoked, and put up his weapon. There was much confusion and jostling, in the midst of which the train moved off. Before the next train, (the following morning) *a new writ from one of*

the Judges of the Supreme Court had been obtained, and Neal was brought back to the city. Just at this junction of affairs, the distinguished Commodore remembered that his broad pendant was floating on the African Squadron, now fitting out at Norfolk, and leaving his victim and his _honor_ behind him, he hastened to rejoin his command. In due course the case was called up, but Commodore Isaac Mayo could nowhere be found, either in his own person, or by counsel, and Neal was discharged. It was fortunate for the Commodore that he was _'non est inventus'._

"4. Now what is the motive for this disgraceful proceeding on the part of the Commodore! The whole charge against Neal, 'the very head and front of his offending' is, that he enticed his wife and children away from slavery. What husband and father would not do the same, and what man is there with flesh in his heart that does not honor the impulse, and bid 'God speed' to the effort! Was it to vindicate Maryland law, Maryland sovereignty, that such a case was trumped up, _three years_ after the fact. The charge itself is unsustained by proof, and based upon the oath of a single slave, on the plantation of the prosecutor. And who may tell what terrible discipline may have wrung from that helpless slave the unwilling oath ! It looks far more like the atrocity of a kidnapper, than the vindication of the right of a sovereign State. The motive was disclosed in the visit of Commodore Mayo to the humble home of Neal, after he had despoiled it of its protector. He had sustained to Neal's wife and her children the same relation that Dr. Morris had to the husband and father. But what *a contrast ! The one putting forth the most earnest and determined efforts to save his freed man, with the purpose full formed and <u>expressed to stand by him here, and in Maryland, and to stand by him to the last</u>. The other, torturing those whose full value he had received, amounting to more than twenty-five hundred dollars. and reveling in their agonies as they writhed in the folds of his mighty malignity. Neal in purchasing his wife and children, and rescuing them from bondage in different States, had thwarted the Commodore's vengeance, or plantation discipline, and he hated him for it. When Neal's wife and children were taken in their attempt to escape from bondage Commodore Mayo gave orders in the sale he soon after made of them, that <u>no two</u> should be sold to the same master. He intended to visit their audacity in that attempt, with a punishment as severe as he could.*

"5. The influence of this disgraceful transaction has been very decided. It has strengthened freedom, and excited deeper hostility to slavery, and a deeper sympathy with the oppressed. I have heard of those among the most influential classes in the city, who could not away with the exaggeration of Mrs. Stowe (Harriet Beacher Stowe), *but who, since this occurrence, have boldly said, that considering all circumstances of the persons, there is nothing in 'Uncle Tom,' in its darkest pictures, more outrageous and atrocious. Of others I have heard, whose blood reached the 'boiling point,' and who demand a petition to the President to dismiss Commodore Mayo from the Navy as a stain and disgrace to it, and to the nation. A petition praying an investigation of the*

case would be largely signed. It is hoped that he will be removed from the command of the African Squadron by the President, as utterly unworthy of occupying a position of such dignity, responsibility and honor.

"Yours," (No name given)

- - - - As you will see in the last chapter, ironically, eight years later, President Lincoln does just that - - - -

We get a Southern point of view:

From the *"Baltimore Sun, Feb. 16th, 1853"* [1d]

"RICHARD NEAL'S CASE – It is not my intention to allow myself to be involved in a newspaper controversy with Richard Neal's abolition allies in Philadelphia or elsewhere.

"An attempt has been made by Dr. Morris, of Philadelphia, to bolster up and sustain a notorious scoundrel and fugitive from justice of this state (Maryland), *who has taken refuge in Philadelphia, which requires being noticed.*

"In an article which appeared in the Philadelphia Bulletin, signed Caspar Morris, and which has since been republished in the Baltimore Sun of the 3rd. inst. under the auspices of G.C. accompanied with comments by that 'humble Quaker', allusion is made at threats against the 'Cheston free negroes', as though 'they were a nuisance', and boldly declares that not one of them has ever been arraigned before a court for violation of laws, &c. The comments accompanying Dr. Morris' letter

betray an intentional suppression of the truth, or gross ignorance of the character and standing of the 'Cheston freed negroes' in this county. For the edification of G.C., I will allude briefly to the more notorious of the gang. John Davis, one of the tribe, was taken in the act of robbery, on Mr. Sheckles' farm, who kindly allowed said Davis to cross his farm, on his way to see his wife, in Annapolis, - - - Davis was arrested, tried and convicted before a Justice of the Peace, and sentenced to be publicly whipped. In consequence of his clearly established guilt, the owner of Davis' wife refused to allow him to visit his home. In 1846 Davis was allowed to re-visit his wife and children, upon promise of good behavior, - - - In the year 1848 Davis enticed and induced his wife and two children, and chancellor Bland's coachman, to run away. The runaways were traced to the Delaware and Chesapeake Canal and seen in the company of John Davis; the slaves have never been heard from since. Has G.C. never seen or heard of a reward of $1,000., then $2,000. and a standing reward of $2,000. for said runaways; also, a reward of $200. for the apprehension of John Davis?

"Shortly after Richard Neal induced his wife and six children to run away; it was learned from a reliable source that Richard Neal aided and assisted John Davis in conveying out of the State sixteen additional slaves.

"Both Richard Neal and John Davis were engaged in the conspiracy which effected the escape of said slaves, the property of Com. Mayo. The same witness alleges that it is the intention of the 'Cheston free negroes' to carry out of the State their wives, if they be slaves.

"Has G.C. forgotten that a slave woman belonging to Mr. C. Weedon, of Anne Arundel County, was secreted by one of the Cheston free; that a law suite was commenced and a jury of twelve men upon their oaths made Mr.S.C. pay dearly for his negro affinities? The Court restored the runaway woman to her master, subsequently this woman ran away from her master and has never been taken.

"It is necessary to refresh G.C.'s doubtful memory with a more recent case. A few months since one of the 'Cheston free negroes' was brought before court for enticing Mr. Hall's slave to run away.

"It would be easy to establish the guilt of the four additional parties of these 'freed negroes', but further notice of the outlaws is deemed unnecessary. - - - From the foregoing the public can judge of the truthfulness of G.C.'s article accompanying Dr. Morris' disingenuous and unfair letter in the Philadelphia Bulletin.

"I will briefly review Dr. Morris' letter to which allusion has been made. It amounts to nothing, and is simply the offspring of a diseased mind, rendered so by the recent proceedings of the mob at Chester, Pa.

"Dr. Morris' statement is based upon information obtained from Richard Neal, because the minuteness with which he alludes to Neal's private concerns, could be known to no one save Neal.

"The Doctor is much astonished at Neal's success, when farming on the island, when contrasted with the Doctor's income from rural pursuits. There is a marked difference between Dr. Morris' system of farming and Richard Neal's. The Doctor works and pays the wages of *free blacks, who steal whatever balance there is on hand at the farm.*

"Dr Morris also states that two slaves were sold by Com Mayo at a certain time mentioned. Why did not the 'learned doctor' state the cause of their being sold? Why has he withheld in his letter the cause? Can it be that it was the slaves were induced to run away by Richard Neal, for whom he manifests so much enthusiastic sympathy and devotion?

"The 'learned doctor' also states that the innocence of Richard Neal can be proved. I presume it could before the same jury who tried the traitors who murdered and butchered the sacred and pure Gorsuch. The evidence submitted to Gov. Lowe, and upon which he issued his requisition, will alone convict Rich'd Neal before an impartial jury.

"After a careful examination of Gov. Lowe's requisition, Gov. Bigler of Pennsylvania issued a warrant to the Sheriff of Philadelphia to surrender the fugitive upon carrying him before a Judge or Alderman, which was complied with. Alderman Kenney gave the case a close investigation and ordered the fugitive into the custody of an officer. If the fugitive be innocent, why did an infuriated mob attempt forcibly his rescue from the officer of the law? Dr. Morris' could have accompanied the prisoner to Maryland, and procured a fair and impartial trial for the prisoner. It is that which they dread, and the consequence of exposures of certain persons, who have thrust themselves into High official positions.

"Dr. Morris' letter contains the most unfounded and prejudice account imaginable of the late proceedings in relation to the arrest and discharge of the fugitive.

"One word concerning the $5,000. advance to enable Neal to purchase his family, &c. It would have been as the Dutchess of Southerland expresses, more charitably expended in relieving the wants of the many poor and friendless Irish and German emigrants, to be met with in Philadelphia, a class of citizens who are under worked by the runaway negroes in the South.

"Dr. Morris also asserts that Neal was arrested for vindictiveness. The assertion is untrue, and unbecoming a gentleman. The reason why the arrest has not been made earlier, is, that Richard Neal's whereabouts has not been made known until very recently.

"In Maryland, where Col. Mayo is known to be a brave, hospitable and generous gentleman, the assaults of his late enemies are regarded as the idle wind which passes by. In conclusion of this statement, it is but fair and proper to state that the agent of Gov. Lowe of Maryland, was obliged to leave Philadelphia, because his <u>life</u> and <u>liberty</u> had been <u>threatened;</u> and before the Governor had time to substitute another agent, Neal was discharged under a writ of habeas corpus, without an examination of the merit of the case.

Annapolis, Feb. 12, 1853" (Writer was not identified).

G.C. - frequently referred to in the above article is Galloway Cheston, brother of Anne (Cheston) Morris, Dr. Caspar Morris' wife.

From Rochester, New York, in the *"Frederick Douglas Paper, February 25, 1853"*: [14]

"THE KIDNAPPERS INDICTED - We find the following paragraph in the 'Delaware Co. Republican', of Saturday last, and hope it is true, though we have not seen the news in any other paper. Perhaps, however, it was contained in the West Chester papers of the previous week, which, owing to our recent illness, did not come under our eye. The hit at the Governor will be understood by those who have heard the private history of his agency in the attempted abduction of Richard Neal: 'The Grand Jury of Chester County, last week, returned a true bill against M'Creary and Merritt, of Elkton, Maryland, for kidnapping Rachael Parker. If Gov. Bigler should refuse to require them to be given up for trial, we hope some one will make the application when he is at a social party - as was the case when he granted the requisition for Richard Neal - and that he will so far forget himself, as to order the Deputy Secretary to issue the writ.' We shall now see whether Gov. Bigler will dare to perform the duty prescribed for him by the laws of the State, or whether he will disregard the action of the Grand Jury and leave the kidnappers to repeat their crime with impunity whenever it may suit their convenience or inclination so to do."*

From Washington D.C. *"The National Era, March 10, 1853"*: [14]

"CASE OF RICHARD NEAL - Much indignation has been aroused against Commodore Isaac Mayo,

of Maryland, lately ordered to the command of the African squadron, on account of his alleged conduct in the case of Richard Neal. According to the newspapers, some years ago the wife and children of Neal, slaves of the Commodore, attempted to escape, but were seized and carried back to their master. He was so incensed against them, according to a correspondent of the New York 'Evangelist', that in the sale he soon afterwards made of them, he gave orders that no two should be sold to the same master. Neal succeeded subsequently in purchasing them all, and rescuing them from bondage. It would seem that the Commodore was not satisfied with this reunion of a family which he had broken up; for, some three years after the attempted escape, a charge was trumped up against Neal, the father, of having been concerned in their abduction. This charge was founded on the oath of a single slave on Mayo's planta-tion - evidence inadmissible against a white man in a Maryland court - and on the strength of it, requisition was made upon Governor Bigler, of Pennsylvania, for the surrender of Neal. He was arrested, and was about being conveyed to Maryland, when a writ of habeas corpus from one of the Judges of the Supreme Court was issued, and Neal was brought back to Philadelphia. 'Just at this junction of affairs (says the correspondent of the New York Evangelist,) the distinguished Commodore remembered that his broad pennant was floating on the African squadron, now fitting out at Norfolk, and leaving his victim and his honor behind him, he hastened to rejoin his command. In due course the case was called up, but Commodore Isaac Mayo could nowhere be found, either in his own person, or by counsel, and Neal was discharged. It was fortunate for the Commodore that he was 'non est inventus.' "If the case be as it is represented, in all the accounts we have seen, the conduct of Commodore Mayo in the transaction is mean and inhuman, and he is the last man who should be selected to uphold the honor of the American flag. If there be another side to the case, he or his friends, in justice to his character, and to the navy, in which he occupies so high a place, should present it without delay."

Richard Neal appears to have lived out the rest of his life as a quiet family man, without further notoriety.

He appeared in the U.S. Federal Census as living in south Philadelphia from 1850 thru 1880. His occupation was listed as a coachman and, last, as a waiter.

Richard and Matilda raised a total of ten children. At least four of the children became teachers. Several of the children eventually returned to live in Anne Arundel County, Maryland.

In the 1880 census record, Richard was listed as a widower, aged 69 with four adult children (all teachers), plus two additional teenager children, all living in his household on Seventh Street. Curiously his son Daniel A. Neal is listed as the census taker.

The following obituaries appeared on August 25, 1881 in "The Christian Recorder" in Philadelphia: [14]

"NEAL - Mr. Richard Neal, of Phila., full asleep in Christ July 28th, at his summer residence, West River, Md."

and:

"NEAL - Miss Matilda H. Neal, the youngest daughter of Richard Neal, fell asleep in Jesus July 25th, at the summer residence, West River, Md."

What tragic occurrence(s) could have taken place three days apart, which would take the lives of a father and his daughter? Where are they buried? These are questions that are still unanswered.

Chapter 13

MAYO'S DEMISE

In 1855, after more than two years at sea, Commodore Mayo is relieved of command of the African Squadron and returned to a quieter life at his plantation and to examining midshipmen at the Naval Academy.

At the approach of the Civil War, a large majority of southern officers, due to family ties and conflicts of interests, chose to resign their commissions and support the Confederacy. It appeared that the senior officer Mayo, who had strong southern sentiment and was the owner of a sizable number of slaves, found it extremely difficult to support the Union.

As Maryland fell under Federal control after a Baltimore mob attacked Federal soldiers, Annapolis was placed under martial law, and Maryland threatened secession from the Union. Mayo submitted his own letter of resignation from the U.S. Navy, to President Lincoln, as follows:

"Gresham
South River, A.A. Co., Md.
May 1st, 1861

"To His Excellency Abraham Lincoln
President of the United States

"I hereby most respectfully tender to you my resigna-
tion of the office of Captain in the United States Navy.
"For more than half a century it has been the pride
of my life to hold office under the Government of the
United States. For twenty-five years I have been engaged
in active service and have never seen my flag dishonored
or the American arms disgraced by defeat. It was the
hope of my old age that I might die, as I had lived, an
officer in the Navy of a free Government. This hope has
been taken from me.
"In adopting the policy of coercion, you have denied
to millions of freemen the rights of the Constitution. In
its stead you have placed the will of a sectional party,
and now demand submission in the name of an armed
force. As one of the oldest soldiers of America, I protest
– in the name of humanity – against this 'war against
brethren.' I cannot fight against the Constitution while
pretending to fight for it.
"You will, therefore, oblige me by accepting my
resignation.
"Most Respectfully, Isaac Mayo
"Captain U.S. Navy Late Commander in Chief of U.S.
Naval Forces, Coast of Africa, Constitution, flagship."

On the reverse of this letter, in response to Captain Mayo's very terse letter, is the notation:

"Dismiss by order the President"

and

"Done May 18, 1861"

Lincoln had allowed between two and three hundred Southern officers to resign honorably at the start of the Civil War.

President Lincoln's response, due to the tenor or tone of Mayo's letter, was simply to scrawl one word - "DISMISS" which meant you did not have the honor of resigning, you're kicked out of the Navy. He was dismissed without military honors.

Mayo took his own life, reportedly the same day of Lincoln's response. He is found dead at "Gresham house" of a gunshot.

Mayo's wife had an obelisk erected in the cemetery at the Naval Academy in his name, although he is not buried there but in a family vault elsewhere in Annapolis at St. Ann's Cemetery. Curiously, the obelisk states that he died May 10th, 1861, while the church records state that he died May 18th, 1861 - the date of Lincoln's response.

It is not until a century and a half latter that a descendent of Commodore Mayo began a twenty-plus-year campaign to try to clear the Commodore's name and restore his honor. Reference: "Naval Warrior: The Life of Commodore Isaac Mayo" by

Byron A. Lee, published by The Anne Arundel County Historical Society in 2002.

There is no doubt that Captain Mayo served his country long and well, and that his name and honor were finally restored by the U.S. Navy.

Mayo Obelisk at U.S. Naval
Academy, Annapolis, MD

APPENDIX

Time Line
Richard Neal
(1810 ± - 1881)

1779   James Cheston Jr. born.

1803   James Cheston Jr. married Mary Ann Hollingsworth.

1805   Casper Morris born at Philadelphia PA, son of Israel W. and Mary (Hollingsworth) Morris.

1810   Ann Cheston born in Ann Arundel County, MD, daughter of James and Ann (Galloway) Cheston.

1810   ± RICHARD NEAL born in Ann Arundel County, MD, parents unknown.

1829   Dr. Casper Morris married Ann Cheston in Baltimore, MD, and lived in a small house on Chestnut Street next to the U.S. Mint in Philadelphia, PA.

1831   Casper & Ann Morris moved to the south side of Chestnut Street, below Broad Street, Philadelphia.

1837±   RICHARD NEAL married MATILDA __??__, a slave of Commodore Isaac Mayo.

1838   William Neal born to Richard & Matilda Neal in Ann Arundel Co., MD.

1839   Rachael Neal born to Richard & Matilda Neal in Ann Arundel Co., MD.

May 31, 1843 - James Cheston Jr. died at age 64.

1844   Distribution of James Cheston's slaves (77) - total value = $14,623.

(12 were manumitted prior to this evaluation, including Richard Neal. All were manumitted prior to the Civil War).

Aug. 6, 1844 - Richard Neal "Manumitted by Casper Morris & wife by deed", among others.

Nov. 10, 1844 - Richard Neal's manumission certificate issued - "Age about 33, 5' - 8 1/2", brown complexion, scar on forehead and right cheek".

1845   Richard Neal works on Dr. Cheston's farm for around a year. He then turned to oystering (digging for oysters), and selling then locally and in Baltimore. He also helped clear land for Richard Carman. He attempted farming on a small island (120 acres) in the South River, owned by Captain Mayo, as a sharecropper for $125 per year for 3 3/4 years.

1846   Mary J. Neal & Emeline Neal (twins?) were born to Richard & Matilda Neal in Anna Arundel Co., MD

1847   Dr. Casper & Ann Morris purchase 1428 Chestnut Street, Philadelphia.

1848   Richard Neal left farming and lived at Gresham for about a year.

1848   James Neal born to Richard & Matilda Neal in Anne Arundel Co., MD.

Fall - 1849   Matilda Neal tired of waiting for freedom and ran away from the Mayo/ Bland plantation at Elk Ridge, MD, with her 5 children and seven other slaves, by water. She and the children were caught in Baltimore. She claimed she had not seen Richard for 3 week before running away.

Commodore Mayo sold Matilda and the 5 children to a slave trader, Mr. Gordon, with the instructions that they were each to be sold separately further south in different states.

Nov. - 1849 Richard feared he would be blamed, and left Maryland to go to Philadelphia to seek advice from Dr. Morris.

He found work there as an ostler (a coach-man/stable hand) for Townsend Sharpless, a wealthy Philadelphia merchant and friend of Dr. Morris

Richard Neal, with the help of Townsend Sharpless, Dr. Casper Morris, and various abolition groups, raised $3,235.68 to purchases Richard's family's freedom.

June - 1850 Richard and his family began living at the Sharpless' property.

1850/53 Presidency of Millard Fillmore upon death of Zachary Taylor.

1850 Richard Neal appeared on the 1850 Federal Census as living in the "Locust Ward" of Philadelphia, age 45, with his wife Matilda - age 35, and children William - age 11, Rachael - age 9, Mary age 7, Emeline age 5, James - age 4, and Kitty age 1.

December 9th, 1852 - Isaac Mayo, Jr. was assigned command of the United States African

Squadron with the USS Constitution as his flagship.

Jan. 20th, 1853 - Thursday Commodore Isaac Mayo Jr. and his slave William Hunter, testified against Richard Neal before Justice of the Peace James Hunter in Maryland .

Jan. 21st, 1853 - Friday. Maryland Gov. Lowe issued a request to PA Gov. Bigler for the arrest of Richard Neal as a fugitive of justice.

Jan. 24th, 1853 - Monday. Pennsylvania Gov. Bigler issued a warrant for Neal's arrest.

January 25, 1853 - Tuesday. Richard Neal was arrested at Mr. Sharpless' stable in Cherry Street around noon, by an officer from Maryland, Mr. Lamb, along with two officers from Philadelphia. Mayo went to Neal's home near 12th and Locust Streets, and told his children to tell their mother, who was working elsewhere, that he had Richard and that "they would never see him again".

Richard was taken to the Courthouse on 5th street, then to the stationhouse below Walnut Street for about an hour and a half. Next, he was taken to an office on South

Street and finally to the Philadelphia, Wilmington and Baltimore train depot where they missed the 2:00 o'clock train by two minutes.

Mayo's party hired a carriage and headed south towards Chester in an attempt to get Richard out of the state as quickly as possible.

In the area of Darby, PA, Richard bolted from the carriage but was recaptured after a lengthy chase, and the party continued to Chester, PA, where they stopped at around 6 p.m. for dinner at "The Goff Hotel", (The Steamboat Hotel owned and operated by John Goff), with the intent of catching the next south-bound train around 11: p.m.

In the meantime, Richard's son, William, went to Dr. Morris's home at 1428 Chestnut Street to seek his help. The doctor was away on a house call. The doctors' teenage son, Galloway Cheston Morris, went to find him.

Upon hearing what was happening, Dr. Morris consulted with the former mayor of Philadelphia and lawyer, Peter McCall, and several other prominent gentlemen. A writ of Habeas Corpus was obtained from the Philadelphia County Court. With the writ in hand, James Cheston Morris, (Galloway's older brother) and others, along with two city policemen, proceed to catch the 10:00 pm train to Chester in hopes of catching up with Mayo's party before they could cross the state line.

When they reached Chester around 11: p.m., they were met at the station by Mayo's party attempting to drag Richard onto the train. There was a confrontation (a "tug of war") between Pro and Anti-slavery parties. The train conductor, Mr. Boucher, became impatient and signaled the engineer to proceed, leaving all parties standing on the station platform.

Richard was taken to the Chester City jail and held overnight chained to the floor. Captain Mayo stood guard all night with a bottle of wine.

Jan. 26th, 1853 - Wednesday. In the morning just before 9 a.m., Mayo and his party took Richard Neal back to the train station at Chester with the intent of continuing their trip south. There, they were met by Dr. Casper Morris, his son, Galloway, a son of Townsend Sharpless, and others with a writ of habeas corpus. Dr. Morris and his party returned to Philadelphia by private coach with Richard Neal. Capt. Mayo returned with them, but was forced to ride outside on the top of the carriage. The rest of Mayo's party returned on the afternoon train.

Jan. 27th, 1853 - Thursday. The hearing began around 11 a.m. before The Supreme Court. The issue now was whether Richard Neal was a "Fugitive of Justice" for enticing his wife and children to run away? There were many legal twists and turns.

Jan. 31, 1853 - Monday. Neither Mayo nor his agent, Mr. Lamb, appeared in court. The Supreme Court found no reason to hold Richard Neal and he was released.

Feb. 4th, 1853 - Friday. Richard Neal has officer Charles Tapper arrested for assault.

A call went out for Capt. Mayo's relief of command.

Feb. 5th, 1853 - Saturday. Sworn affidavits were taken from Richard, Matilda, William and Rachel Neal, witnessed by Charles Gilpin, mayor of Philadelphia.

1861 - 1865 - Presidency of Abraham Lincoln

May 18th, 1861 - Commodore Mayo chose not to support the Union in the Civil War. In a letter to President Lincoln, Mayo asked to be allowed to resign. Lincoln did not accept Mayo's resignation and, instead, ordered his dismissal from the Navy.

On that same day Commodore Mayo was found dead of a gunshot wound at his residence, "Gresham", in Edgewater, Maryland.

Aug. 25, <u>1881</u> - Obituaries - The Christian Recorder, Philadelphia, PA.

"Mr. *Richard Neal*, of Phila., full asleep in Christ July 28th, at his summer residence, West River, Md."

also

"Miss Matilda H. *Neal*, the youngest daughter of *Richard Neal*, fell asleep in Jesus July 25th, at the summer residence, West River, Md.

Bibliography/Sources/References/Credits

[1.]   The author's personal Morris / Cheston family archives.

a. Family letters, transcripts and notes.
b. Photographs from Galloway C. Morris glass negatives.
c. Transcripts of Neal family affidavits - Feb. 5th, 1853.
d. Original 1853 newspaper articles.
e. Richard Neal's original manumission paper.

[2.]   <u>Letter - July 13th 1896</u> - Galloway Cheston Morris to Lawrence J. Morris - Reaney Kelly Collections, MS. 1970 - Maryland Historical Society.

[3.]   <u>Biographical Sketch of CASPAR MORRIS, M. D.</u> by J. Cheston Morris, M.D., College of Physicians of Philadelphia, Nov. 2, 1887. - author's archives.

[4.]   Map - www.historicmapworks.com/
        MAP/US/18312/Anne+Arundel+County

[5.]   Caspar Morris home - Philadelphia,
        "Philadelphia Then and Now" The
        Philadelphia Inquirer - Oct. 13, 1935.

[6.]   Commodore Mayo: A man of adventure and
        tragedy - by Jonathan Pitts. The Baltimore
        Sun - May 14, 2011.

[7.]   http://en.wikipedia.org/
        wiki/Isaac_Mayo.

[8.]   Newspaper photographs - Goff Hotel and
        Train Station at Chester PA. Courtesy
        of Delaware County Historical Society,
        Chester, PA.

[9.]   Painting - Commodore Isaac Mayo - 1838
        - attributed to Benjamin West, Maryland
        State Archives.

[10.]   Old Ironsides - An Illustrated History of
        USS Constitution. by Thomas P. Horgan

[11.]   Historical Society of Pennsylvania,
        Philadelphia, PA.

[12.]   Chester County Historical Society, West
        Chester, PA.

[13.]   The Quaker Collection, Haverford College, Haverford, PA.

[14.]   Courtesy M. Jerrado, Mother Bethel AME Church, Philadelphia, PA.

ACKNOWLEDGEMENTS

F irst and foremost to my ancestors, without whose penchant for hording ephemera, this historical narrative could not have been written today.

To my mentor Michael T.S. Payton - historian and lecturer, who encouraged me to go forth with this project, and assisted me time and again with research.

To the Historical Society of Pennsylvania, Chester County Historical Society, Delaware County Historical Society, Friends Historical Library of Swarthmore College, Quaker Library of Haverford College, and The Library Company of Philadelphia, who freely opened their libraries and assisted me with my research.

To numerous organizations and residents of the Galesville area of Anne Arundel County, Maryland, including the Galesville Heritage Society, Smithsonian Environmental Research Center, Elinor L. Thompson - genealogist, author and historian, John Colhoun, Anne Franke, Gertrude E. Makell and Addison Worthington.

Lastly to my wife, Mary Jane, and to Eve Webb for helping to make this narrative legible.